Golf Gadgets:
Cool Stuff You Never Knew You Needed

Sports Publishing, Inc.
www.SportsPublishingInc.com

Layout and design: Erin J. Prescher
Cover design: Scot Muncaster
Editor: Susan M. McKinney

Pictures provided courtesy of Dreaming Dog Group

ISBN:1-58382-014-0
Library of Congress Catalog Card Number: 99-60969

Sports Publishing, Inc.
804 N. Neil St.
Champaign, IL 61820
www.SportsPublishingInc.com

Table of Contents

Acknowledgments iv

Introduction v

Hole 1 1

Hole 2 10

Hole 3 18

Hole 4 26

Hole 5 37

Hole 6 45

Hole 7 53

Hole 8 63

Hole 9 71

Hole 10 80

Hole 11 90

Hole 12 100

Hole 13 111

Hole 14 121

Hole 15 128

Hole 16 135

Hole 17 143

Hole 18 146

Acknowledgments

We pay tribute to the unknown creators of the countless golf jokes that make the rounds, as well as others who supplied quips and tips.

Thanks to Tom Bast and Tom Doherty of Sportsmasters, Peter Bannon and Mike Pearson of Sports Publishing Inc. Also thank you to Susan M. McKinney, Erin J. Prescher and Scot Muncaster.

Introduction

Golf isn't a sport. It isn't a game. And it most definitely isn't a hobby.

It's a passion for the millions of players who call themselves golfers. Obsessed? Maybe. Possessed? Likely.

Once hooked, golfers find it difficult to go halfway. The search is on for perfection in a passion that will not allow for it. Perfection is for philosophers to debate. Golfers are just trying to get a small white ball into a hole.

Because of the imperfections, golfers must maintain a proper perspective. A bit of humor here and a dig there, well timed between an outburst here and a thrown club there. Golfers come in all ages, all races and both sexes. Rich and poor. Scratch players and hackers. Few activities span as wide a spectrum.

However, all golfers are alike in one way. Each seeks any equipment, swing technique or mental trick that gets the ball into the hole in fewer shots than yesterday's round or the previous hole.

This book is for golfers who are passionate. You are an immediate qualifier. You are, after all, reading this.

This book attempts to give golfers the edge—any edge—in becoming better players. There is information about new clubs and other golf equipment. There are swing aids and golf gifts. The golf industry never is at a loss for new items.

There also are some playing tips. Every golfer relishes a good tip, no matter how small or how often it has been heard. That one new tip might be the difference between a double-bogey and a par. Or between a par and a birdie.

And there also are some laughs. Golf jokes—some old, some new—and quips from some of golf's most interesting personalities.

We hope it all makes for an interesting round of reading and an interesting round the next time you tee it up.

D avid Leadbetter is considered by many to be the No. 1 golf instructor in the world. His students include Nick Faldo, Nick Price, David Frost, Larry Mize and Brad Faxon. He has a whole product line of instructional aids covering the full swing, short game and putting (as well as a collection of hats).

"The Right Link" is billed as a game improvement tool that automatically places the right arm in the correct position throughout the golf swing. Made of hard plastic, foam padding and a series of Velcro straps, "The Right Link" retails for about $40.

Says Leadbetter: "I believe that the right arm is the most misunderstood element of the golf swing and that the move-away is vital to consistent shot making. 'The Right Link' will give you the proper

move-away, set you at the top of the swing, and give you that perfect release position at impact that all golfers want. It will improve your rhythm, plus practicing with 'The Right Link' regularly will automatically improve your muscle memory, and when you remove it, your swing will become an instinctive movement."

It is designed to position the right arm (for right-handed swingers) at 90 degrees at the top of the back swing to eliminate over swinging. It teaches the correct move-away in the back swing in order to hinge the club properly. It provides width in the swing in order to promote shot making and encourages a proper release from the top of the back swing.

Other products in the line include (with the company's description):

"The Coach." It is the only fitness and training system designed to improve your game quickly. In only 12 minutes a day, three times a week, you will start hitting the ball longer and straighter while developing a better swing. You'll become stronger and more flexible while working on your swing. The correct swing will feel natural . . . like it's always been part of your game. ($379.95)

"ComputerCoach." Used by Leadbetter with his tour players and at his teaching facilities, it is golf's most advanced swing analysis system. It merges the effectiveness of video with the power and speed of the computer. ($495)

"The Glove." Use this specially marked glove to grip the club exactly as Leadbetter instructs his pupils. It teaches you while you play. ($18.95)

"The Targaline." It is designed to teach a golfer to see the line of a putt. It features a target line string that shows how to visualize the ball's path to the target. It also incorporates a ball-eye alignment mirror for proper head positioning, as well as stroke-path markings to teach squared putter face positioning. ($79.95)

"The Mirror." It provides a wide field of vision and has a vertical cross hair that enables you to see subtle swing characteristics. Check the links in your swing and add confidence to your game at home or on the range. ($24.95)

"The Magic Eye." Place it in front of your stance and check your body positioning during the address, back swing and down-swing positions. Develop proper

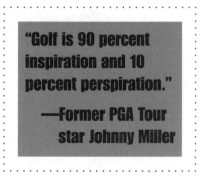

"Golf is 90 percent inspiration and 10 percent perspiration."

—Former PGA Tour star Johnny Miller

shoulder turn and weight transfer. Eliminate excessive up and down body movement. ($21.95)

"The Set Right." Just snap two clubs together and begin your practice. The connector forms a T that helps align any golfer in the proper stance. ($7.95)

"The Power Link." Based on The Right Link, it keeps the right arm in the proper position throughout the swing to help generate power and eliminate any over swinging. ($19.95)

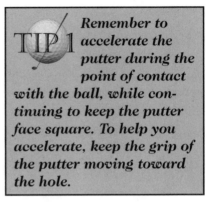

TIP 1 *Remember to accelerate the putter during the point of contact with the ball, while continuing to keep the putter face square. To help you accelerate, keep the grip of the putter moving toward the hole.*

"The Short Club." Now you can actually feel and learn what videos are teaching you. Don't just watch—act out the drills while you watch. It is only 27 inches long, so you won't have to worry about using it indoors. ($21.95)

"The Putting Rules." Developed by Leadbetter to help you make a more consistent putting stroke. It is 36 inches long for easy storage in your golf bag and comes with simple, easy-to-use drills and 10 putting secrets from Leadbetter. ($24.95)

"The Putting Necklace." Learn and feel the proper putting stroke used by Tour players. It teaches the pendulum putting method for a more consistent and accurate stroke. Includes an instructional video. ($19.95)

Golf Training Systems, Inc. is based in Duluth, Georgia, (770) 623-6400.

*D*uring the weekly Lamaze class, the instructor emphasized the importance of exercise, hinting strongly that husbands need to get out and start walking with their wives.

From the back of the room one expectant father inquired, "Would it be okay if she carries a bag of golf clubs while she walks?"

*T*he judge asked the defendant golfer to please stand. "You are charged with murdering a caddie with a 3-wood."

From out in the gallery, a man shouts, "Liar!"

"Silence in the court!" the judge says to the man who shouted. He turns to the defendant golfer and says, "You are also charged with killing a clubhouse attendant with a putter."

"Tightwad" the same man in the gallery blurted out.

"I said QUIET!" yelled the judge. To the defendant golfer he said, "You are also charged with killing an assistant pro with your 5-iron."

"You jerk!" the man from the gallery yelled.

The judge thundered at the man in the gallery, "If you don't tell me right now the reasons for your outbursts, I'll hold you in contempt!"

The man answered back, "I've lived beside that man for ten years now, but do you think he ever had a golf club when I needed to borrow one?"

*R*ick Smith, dubbed "Golf's Newest Superstar Teacher" has a training aid named "Right Angle2." The principle is similar to Leadbetter's "The Right Link."

The "Right Angle2" is designed to automatically teach you to extend the take away long and low as you start your swing. It prohibits collapsing (over bending) the right arm at the top of your back swing. It

automatically places your arm in the proper position, creating extension and power through impact. It also teaches you through feel and sound the correct release of the right arm and club head on the downswing. It automatically eliminates your slice and promotes a draw. And finally, it eliminates an incomplete follow through. You will feel a complete extension toward the target after impact.

Its construction and materials are almost identical to Leadbetter's "The Right Link."

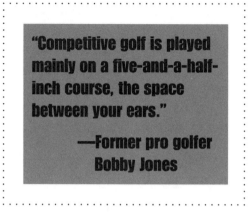

> "Competitive golf is played mainly on a five-and-a-half-inch course, the space between your ears."
>
> —Former pro golfer Bobby Jones

The "Right Angle2" retails for about $50. It is a Rick Smith Signature Training Product and distributed by Corder Enterprises of Anderson, South Carolina, (803) 224-0066.

*M*ark was an avid golfer.
He played golf every chance he got; in the rain, in the cold; he even used black balls to play when there was snow on the ground.

His wife joked, half in jest, that she was a golf widow, and she really wouldn't miss her husband all that much if he died before her, for he was never around anyhow.

He spent all his spare money on golf items and gadgets; trick exploding balls, tees with no indentation on the top so the golf ball would roll off it, towels with witty golf sayings on them and all kinds of golf hats.

One night he was in bed asleep after having played 36 holes of golf that day. He was tired, but he dreamed, replaying the whole round.

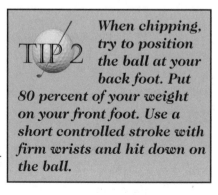

When chipping, try to position the ball at your back foot. Put 80 percent of your weight on your front foot. Use a short controlled stroke with firm wrists and hit down on the ball.

Suddenly his dream was interrupted by the appearance of an angel. It was an angel like he had seen in Bible drawings and other artwork depicting angels. He was instantly awakened.

The angel, with a full set of wings and wearing a long flowing white robe, stood at the foot of his bed.

"Mark?" the angel asked.

"Yes, what is it? You are an angel, aren't you?" Mark asked.

"Of course, I'm an angel. You don't think I'd normally walk around in this silly costume, do you? In fact, I'm your guardian angel," the angel said.

"Does that mean I get three wishes?" Mark asked.

"No, I'm not that kind of guardian angel," the heavenly being answered. "As you know, Mark, you are getting on in years and you don't have as much time left on earth as you once did. Although I can't grant wishes for you, I can answer questions you might have about the hereafter. You do believe in the hereafter, don't you, Mark?"

"Oh yes, and I've been good, with maybe the possible exception of having played too much golf in my lifetime," Mark replied.

"Playing golf is like going fishing," replied the angel. "There is no such thing as playing too much golf or going fishing too often. Do you have any questions about heaven?"

"As a matter of fact, I do," said Mark. "I've often wondered if there are any golf courses in heaven. Can you answer that for me?"

"Gee, Mark, no one ever has asked me that question before. I'll have to go back and check on it. Go back to sleep, and I'll be back in 30 minutes."

With that, the angel disappeared. Mark rubbed his eyes and opened them again. The angel was gone and Mark wondered if he had just had a weird dream. He rolled over on his side and was soon snoring softly again.

True to his word, the angel reappeared within 30 minutes.

"Mark!" the angel called.

Mark woke up to see the angel again standing at the foot of his bed.

"Oh, you're back."

"Yes, Mark, I'm back and I have the answer to your question. But before I tell you, I have to advise that the answer is in two parts, good news and bad news. Which do you want first?"

"Oh, dear, I suppose give me the good news first," responded Mark.

"OK, the good news is there are golf courses in heaven. All the courses have been designed by Arnold Palmer, Pete Dye and Jack Nicklaus. There are no greens fees and electric carts are provided at no charge. You have the choice of any brand of clubs you desire. Each course has 36 holes. The greens are always freshly mowed; the sand traps freshly raked; the roughs aren't too high; and you never lose a ball in the water because the balls float. When you hit a ball into the woods it always ricochets back into the middle of the fairway. And on every par-3 hole you will score a hole-in-one. Yes, you will have a wonderful time playing golf in heaven."

"Oh, that sounds wonderful. With all that good news what could the bad news possibly be?" Mark wondered.

"The bad news is you have a nine o'clock tee time tomorrow morning."

*T*he English teacher was taking her first golfing lesson. "Is the word spelled P-U-T or P-U-T-T?" she asked. "P-U-T-T is correct," her instructor replied. "P-U-T means to place a thing where you want it. P-U-T-T means merely a vain attempt to do the same thing."

*A*nother teaching vehicle taking the place of standard videotapes is instructional CD-ROMs. Golf by IntelliMedia is an interactive CD-ROM that gives you live action videos, superb graphics and personalized instruction from golf's all-time leading money winner, Tom Kite.

Through the use of live-action video and graphics, the two CD-ROM-set includes lessons from Kite and tips from sports psychologist Dr. Bob Rotella.

It's available for $59.95 (plus shipping and handling) from Affordable Golf of Virginia Beach, Virginia, (757) 425-GOLF.

> **TIP 3** *Don't try to make miracle shots when you are in trouble. When in doubt, play it safe. The chance to make par and ending up with a bogey is much better than a double-bogey—or worse.*

*I*t was a sunny Saturday morning, and Joe was beginning his pre-shot routine, visualizing his coming shot when a voice came over the clubhouse loudspeaker.

"Would the gentleman on the ladies' tee please back up to the men's tee, please?"

Joe was still deep in his routine, seemingly impervious to the interruption.

The call came again. "Would the man on the ladies' tee kindly back up the men's tee? Now!"

Joe had had enough.

He shouted, "Would the announcer in the clubhouse kindly shut up and let me play my second shot!"

Slicers sometimes can get an easy cure for their problems with an Anti-Slice Tee. Gold Eagle Professional Golf Products of Dallas, Texas, makes plastic "cup" tees that prevent the ball from flying wildly.

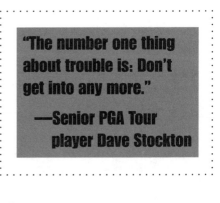

"The number one thing about trouble is: Don't get into any more."

—Senior PGA Tour player Dave Stockton

The tee does not allow the club face to touch the ball; therefore, the ball leaves the tee without spin, theoretically reducing the distance the ball will travel off-course.

> TIP 4
>
> *A missed putt usually will tell you the correct line for your next putt, so always watch the ball until it comes to a rest.*

The tees are available at most golf stores for $1.99 for a package of four.

*O*ne Sunday morning, a priest looks out his window at a beautiful, sunny day.

Although he knows that it's his responsibility to say Mass in an hour he calls in, complaining of illness.

He then sneaks out the back door with his golf clubs.

Up in heaven, St. Peter and God are watching.

St. Peter says to God, "You can't let that go unpunished! That priest is giving in to temptation and not living up to his vows."

God agrees, but as St. Peter watches, the priest is having the round of his life. In fact, on the par-3 16th hole, the priest hits a beautiful shot and the ball rolls into the hole for his first ever hole-in-one.

St. Peter is very upset and says to God, "Do something! He's having the round of his life!"

God calmly turns to St. Peter, smiles and says, "Yes, but who's he going to tell?"

"Golf is twenty percent mechanics and technique. The other eighty percent is philosophy, humor, tragedy, romance, melodrama, companionship, camaraderie, cussedness and conversation."

—Famed sportswriter Grantland Rice

HOLE 2

Gold Eagle of Dallas also makes a number of other inexpensive golf accessories. Among the most handy is the Putter Prop. Instead of using a tee, you can use the Prop to keep any club off the wet grass by elevating the grip. A clip prevents the club from slipping, unlike using a tee. The Putter Prop costs $1.99.

The Tee-Gar is an attachment to any wooden tee that will hold a golfer's cigar while he takes his turn to hit. According to the package, the Tee-Gar helps prevent unwanted flavors associated with fertilizers, pesticides and dirt. It also doubles as a club prop. The Tee-Gar sells for $3.49 at most discount golf stores.

The Range Finder is a small plastic viewer that fits into your shirt or pants pocket. It estimates the distance from the ball to the pin, from 50 to 220 yards. You simply site the pin through the view finder, fit the flag between the top broken line in the viewer and the

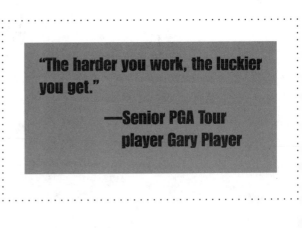

"The harder you work, the luckier you get."

—Senior PGA Tour player Gary Player

solid line below and read the distance. It also has a built-in scorekeeper. All for just $4.49.

A guy's wife constantly berated him to teach her to play golf.

Finally, one morning he relented. Off they went. First hole: par 3, 179 yards, very pretty.

Husband steps up first and says, "Now watch me, and do the same thing."

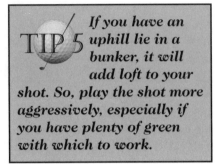

If you have an uphill lie in a bunker, it will add loft to your shot. So, play the shot more aggressively, especially if you have plenty of green with which to work.

A nice shot, lands on the green with about 30 feet to the cup.

Wife steps up, drills it, hooks it, and bounces it off a rock, clips a tree, sideswipes the second rock and rolls up onto the green and goes into the hole.

Husband looks at this, and says, "OK, now you know how to play; let's go home."

. . . .

A foursome watches a lone player play up short of the green they are on.

As they tee off at the next hole they watch the lone player quickly chip on and putt out.

He almost runs to the tee where the group is. He looks at the bewildered players and says, "I say, chaps, could I play through? I've just heard the wife has had a terrible accident."

After paying $450 for an oversized driver, how are you assured that it will be protected from normal airplane luggage wear and tear while it is in a canvas travel bag? There are no more worries if you get the Club Saver. The sturdy black plastic case protects one club of your choice, then fits back into your golf bag. It is big enough to hold any driver on the market today. It retails for about $30.

JWT Associates, Inc. is based in Indianapolis.

A man played a round of golf with a nice young fellow.
On the first hole, which was a long par four with water to the right and a deep ravine to the left, the young man took out a brand new sleeve of balls, teed one up and immediately hit it into the water on the right.

Undaunted, he pulled another ball from the sleeve and hit that one into the ravine, as well.

TIP 6 *Don't automatically tee the ball in the center of the tee box. Pick the spot where you can set-up your stance most comfortably. Make sure there aren't any obstacles, such as overhanging limbs, blocking your shot. If you have a tendency to fade your drives, tee up on the right side of the box and aim for the left edge of the fairway. If you usually draw, then tee up on the left side and aim for the right side of the fairway.*

Then he took the last ball from the sleeve and hit it, too, into the water.

He then reached into his bag and pulled out another brand new sleeve of balls.

"Why don't you hit an old ball?" he was asked.

The response: "I've never had an old ball."

> **"If you want to beat someone out on the golf course, just get him mad."**
>
> **—Dave Williams**

O K, so you spent all that money for a Taylor Made Burner Bubble Driver. You have the cool black and copper head cover and a matching black bag. What do you need to complete the look? How about a Taylor Made Burner towel?

That's right. For $12.99 you can get a bag towel that looks exactly like the head cover. Get one from Golf Circuit at (800) 785-4653.

Joe and his priest are playing in a golf match.

Joe's game is perfect that day, and he is giving the priest a thorough drubbing.

The priest can only sigh as he fills in the scorecard from the last hole.

Sensing his pastor's unhappiness, Joe says to him, "Cheer up Father. Just think, one of these days you will be giving the services at my funeral."

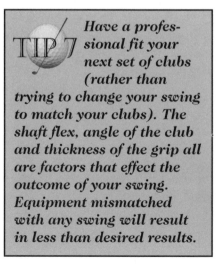

TIP 7 Have a professional fit your next set of clubs (rather than trying to change your swing to match your clubs). The shaft flex, angle of the club and thickness of the grip all are factors that effect the outcome of your swing. Equipment mismatched with any swing will result in less than desired results.

The priest looked at him and made a poor attempt at a grin while saying, "Yes, that may be true, but it will still be your hole."

· · · · · · · · · · · ·

*J*esus and Moses were playing golf one day.
They arrived at a tough, 215-yard, par-three, all over water.
Jesus had the honor and stepped up to the tee with a 4 iron. Moses tried to convince him that it wasn't the right club, "That's not enough club; you need at least a 4 wood."

Jesus responded, "No, I saw Arnold Palmer play this hole the other day and he put a 4 iron five feet from the pin and sank the putt for a birdie."

Moses said, "I'm telling you, that's not enough club!"

Jesus hit the ball into the water. He parted the water, walked out and got the ball, smoothed out the water and teed up again.

Moses said, "I told you that was not enough club; you need at least a 4 wood."

Jesus said, "This will be fine; remember what I said about Arnold Palmer."

Jesus hit the ball into the water one more time. As Moses looked on in disgust, Jesus got his ball and teed it up for yet another try. About that time the next foursome was approaching the tee and one of the golfers in the new foursome said, "What's he doing hitting a 4 iron on this hole? He needs at least a 4 wood. Who does he think he is, Jesus Christ?"

"No," replied Moses, "He thinks he's Arnold Palmer!"

*I*f you prefer to walk and carry your own golf bag, then listen to the story of Warren Sattler.

"It was on the fourteenth hole that my drive took a surprisingly hard left turn into the trees. I grabbed my clubs and started off to look for my ball. Besides hitting the perfect duck hook, what happened on that shot? The answer came to me as I shifted my golf bag from my right to my left shoulder. My clubs were getting heavy, and I was tired.

"If given a choice, I prefer to walk. It's simply the best way to play the game of golf. I'm never quite into my game if I ride in a golf cart, and pulling a bag cart doesn't suit me. A caddie would be great, but such a luxury is a rarity. So I carry my clubs in one of those lightweight carry bags. But even with the lightweight bag, by the middle of the back nine, my clubs get heavy. I found that I often alternated shoulders to relieve the strain.

"Then the idea hit. Why can't there be a second strap for the other shoulder? When worn with the usual single carry strap, the weight of the bag would balance out between both shoulders.

"It would have to go on and come off easily. It would have to work equally well for the golfer who normally carries his or her bag on the left shoulder and for the golfer who prefers the bag on the right shoulder. It would have to work without modifying the golf bag. It would have to fit any size golfer, male or female. And, it would have to leave the bag manufacturer's original carry strap intact.

"The last feature is of great importance. Often—far too often for most of us—clubs are carried for very short distances. The golf bag goes on and comes off frequently. Golf is not a five-mile hike with a backpack! For those short hauls, you want to carry your bag as originally designed, well balanced with the existing carry strap.

"With thankful editorial input from friends and my sister (she's a 5 handicapper!) The Strap was created to meet the needs of the golfer who packs his or her bag—or who would like to, but thinks the extra effort is too much. I am certain that you will find this simple, yet unique, shoulder strap a surprisingly effective solution for improving the quality of golf only experienced by walking the course."

With that, The Strap was developed by Sattler.

The Strap, which sells for about $20, is a combination of foam padding and Velcro straps. It takes just a minute to attach it to your bag, but a couple of minutes longer to get the balance adjusted. It also takes some practice finding the opening for your arm without looking back as well as shrugging it into place. However, after a couple of holes you'll wonder why the two-shoulder strap isn't standard gear for every golf bag.

The Strap is made by Bag-Pakkers, Inc. in Menlo Park, California, and distributed by Highlander Golf.

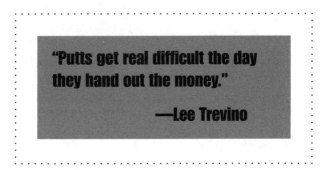

"Putts get real difficult the day they hand out the money."

—Lee Trevino

*M*ember: *Well, caddie, how do you like my game?*
Caddie: *Very good, sir! But personally, I prefer golf.*

· · · · · · · · · · · ·

Member: *Notice any improvement in my game, caddie?*
Caddie: *Shined your clubs?*

· · · · · · · · · · · ·

Member: *Well, I have never played this badly before!*
Caddie: *I didn't realize you had played before, sir!*

· · · · · · · · · · · ·

Member: *Caddie, do you think my game is improving?*
Caddie: *Oh, yes, sir! You miss the ball much closer than you used to!*

Member: My wife says if I don't stop playing golf, she's going to leave me!
Caddie: I'm sure you'll miss her terribly, sir!

. . . .

Member: Please stop checking your watch all the time, caddie. It's distracting!
Caddie: This isn't a watch, sir. It's a compass!

*T*wo guys are waiting at the fourth tee on a warm summer day watching a golfer look for his ball along the shore of a large lake adjacent to the fairway. Suddenly the golfer falls in the lake and is under the water for quite some time.

"Hey, we have to get that guy out before he drowns!" one of them says. So both guys jump in the water and start searching frantically. Finally they find a limp body and swim it to shore.

"This guy has swallowed water. We have to give him CPR."

So one of the guys starts giving him CPR. After a couple of minutes he looks up and says, "Wow, this guy has bad breath! I can't continue this."

So the other guy says, "Well, get out of the way then. I can't let him die."

The second guy starts CPR. A couple of minutes later he also stops and says, "You're right, he sure does have bad breath."

The first guy says, "Something is funny here. Wasn't the guy that we were watching wearing golf shoes?"

"Yeah..." responds the other guy, "so how come this guy is wearing ice skates?"

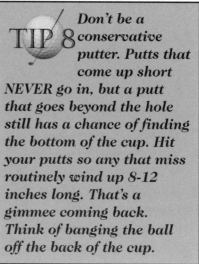

TIP 8 *Don't be a conservative putter. Putts that come up short NEVER go in, but a putt that goes beyond the hole still has a chance of finding the bottom of the cup. Hit your putts so any that miss routinely wind up 8-12 inches long. That's a gimmee coming back. Think of banging the ball off the back of the cup.*

HOLE 3

A pair of Synthetic Winter Golf Gloves makes playing in cold weather more comfortable. Wear two gloves. The palms are made of the same leather material that most golf glove manufacturers use. The back of the gloves, though, are made of acrylic knit which will keep your hands warm in virtually any weather condition. The gloves are easy to get on and off with a Velcro tab.

Valley Forge Sports, Inc. of Broomall, Pennsylvania, makes the gloves for $13.99 a pair. For more information, call (610) 543-4690.

After being away from home for three months trying to make it on the European tour, the golf pro was finally back in bed with his wife, hoping to make up for lost time.

Later in the evening when they were asleep, there was a loud knock at the door, and they both sat up straight. "My God, that must be your hus-

TIP 9 On chip shots, your hands should remain ahead of the ball at impact. Do not try to get the ball in the air by scooping at it. Get the ball on the green as easily as possible and allow for the roll.

band!" exclaimed the golf pro.

"No, it can't be," said his wife. "He's in Europe playing golf."

*M*ilt stood over his tee shot on the eighteenth hole for what seemed like forever.

He'd waggle, look down, look up, waggle, look down, look up, but would never start his back swing.

Finally, Herb, his playing partner, asked, "Why on earth are you taking so long to make this shot?"

"My wife is up there watching me from the clubhouse, and I want to make this shot a good one," said Milt.

"Good Lord," said Herb. "You ain't got a chance of hitting her from here."

*S*ave the strain on your back from stooping to pick up your ball out of the hole. Get a Ball Pick-Up.

For just $1.50 you can get a rubber suction cup that fits on the end of the grip of most putters. After sinking a putt, stick the end your putter into the hole, press firmly on the ball and *viola*, the ball is recovered without any back strain.

The Ball Pick-Up is made by JP Lann

Golf and distributed by Nefouse Enterprises, Inc. of Royal Oak, Michigan.

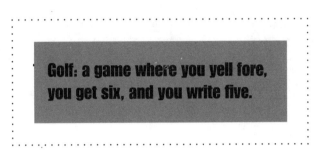

Golf: a game where you yell fore, you get six, and you write five.

*O*ne morning, a gentleman hit a horrible slice off the first tee. He threw his driver back into the bag and proceeded toward the wooded area where he thought his shot had entered.

Shortly after entering the woods, he noticed he was coming upon the fence surrounding the golf course. On the other side of the fence was a road with numerous police, fire and ambulances attending what looked like an overturned school bus. The golfer stopped at the fence, called over a bystander and inquired, "What in heaven's name happened here?"

The answer brought chills up the golfer's back as he was told that it looked as though a small round object had crashed through the driver's window; striking the driver in the forehead and causing instant death.

Unfortunately, that was not the worst.

Several students riding on the bus had been critically injured with multiple fractures and two small children had been found thrown from the bus and were pronounced dead at the scene.

The golfer was in a state of shock, and without saying a

TIP 10 Always keep your club faces clean. The grooves on irons are there for a reason—to provide better control of the shot. Don't forget to clean your putter blade, too. Mud or grass can cause a mishit.

word, quickly and quietly turned and headed for the clubhouse before anyone suspected him of this horrible tragedy.

Upon arriving at the clubhouse, he knew he could not hold this secret inside and looked for an official of the club. No one seemed to be around except the club pro in the pro shop.

Without hesitation, the golfer threw open the door to the pro shop, ran in and stated, "I sliced off of No. 1 and the ball went through a school bus window and it killed the driver, critically injured several students and caused the death of two young students! What in heaven's name do I do now?"

The pro replied, "You might try either closing the club face a bit or moving your back leg in the direction you want the ball to travel!"

* * * * * * * * * * * * *

E laine Johnson, after her shot ricocheted off a tree into her bra: "I'll take the 2-stroke penalty, but I'll be damned if I play it where it lies."

T o avoid arthritis pain, several players suggest copper bracelets. They come in a variety of sizes, styles and prices.

According to the package for a copper bracelet from Seville, "Consistent medicinal use of copper has been recorded throughout history. The ancient Egyptians, Greeks, Romans and Modern Day Man have experienced the benefits of copper and do not hesitate to exalt its results."

It also says, "A greenish stain will likely appear on your wrist.

Don't worry, it is caused by your body's acidity and you may wash it off when you bathe."

Seville's Lexis model retails for about $13. It is produced by Seville Enterprises, Inc. based in Sikeston, Missouri, (573) 472-1997.

A *guy is stranded on a desert island, all alone for 10 years. One day, he sees a speck on the horizon. He thinks to himself, It's not a ship.*

The speck gets a little closer and he thinks, It's not a boat.

The speck gets even closer and he thinks, It's not a raft.

Then, out of the surf comes a gorgeous blonde woman, wearing a wet suit and scuba gear.

She comes up to the guy and says, "How long has it been since you've had a cigarette?"

"Ten years," he screams.

She reaches over and unzips a waterproof pocket on her left sleeve and pulls out a pack of fresh cigarettes. He takes one, lights it, takes a long drag, and says, "Man, oh, man! Is that good!"

Then she asked, "How long has it been since you've had a drink of whiskey?"

He replies, "Ten years!"

She reaches over, unzips her waterproof pocket on her right sleeve, pulls out a flask and gives it to him. He takes a long swig and says, "Wow, that's fantastic!"

Then she starts unzipping this long zipper that runs down the front of her wet suit and she says to him, "And how long has it been since you've had some real fun?"

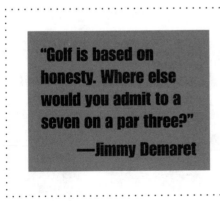

"Golf is based on honesty. Where else would you admit to a seven on a par three?"

—Jimmy Demaret

And the man replies, "My God! Don't tell me that you've got golf clubs in there!"

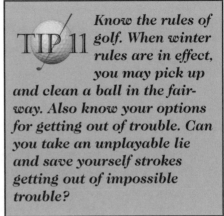

TIP 11 *Know the rules of golf. When winter rules are in effect, you may pick up and clean a ball in the fairway. Also know your options for getting out of trouble. Can you take an unplayable lie and save yourself strokes getting out of impossible trouble?*

Most teaching pros at local golf clubs utilize a swing machine to help players "feel" the plane of the swing. The plastic circle and stand are adjustable to suit virtually any size golfer, and can be used by both right- and left-handed players.

The Mad Jack Swing Machine Training System is designed by John Alexander, an engineer. It helps golfers feel the proper full, fluid swing. The machine trains your muscles to remember the right elliptical path your club has to travel to hit accurate shots consistently.

The Swing Machine is made by Mad Jack Golf, Inc. of Springfield, Illinois, and retails for $299.95. For more information, call (888) 294-4708.

A man playing as a single at Pebble Beach was teamed with a twosome. After a few holes, the twosome finally asked why he was playing such a beautiful course by himself.

He replied that he and his wife had played the course every year for over 20 years, but this year she had passed away. He kept the tee time in her memory.

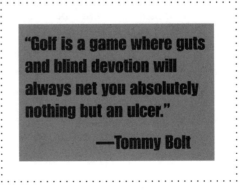

"Golf is a game where guts and blind devotion will always net you absolutely nothing but an ulcer."

—Tommy Bolt

The twosome commented that this was very thoughtful, indeed, but certainly someone would have been willing to take her spot.

"I thought so, too," he replied, "but they all wanted to go to the funeral."

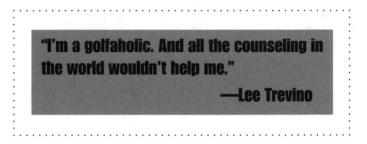

"I'm a golfaholic. And all the counseling in the world wouldn't help me."

—Lee Trevino

*T*hree pals always were trying new venues.

On a crisp, clear Saturday morning, they were teeing off at yet another golf club from the No. 1 box. The hole was a par 4 with water hugging the fairway halfway down the left side.

Of course, one of them hit into the lake. They all headed to find the ball.

Since they weren't extremely accomplished players, each used different equipment to get their balls back. They pulled in an old lantern and began to rotate it. A genie appeared and said each man would be granted one wish.

The first said he wanted fabulous wealth. All of a sudden, there were millions in gold bars at his feet.

The second wanted to have his way with the women. Instantly, he felt the necessary confidence and courage.

The third? Well, after a bit of thought, he stammered that he wanted to be God. In a flash, he looked down at the front of his cardigan, where he found a brass name tag, on which was inscribed: John Smith, Rules Committee Chairman.

TIP 12 *Take note of any divot you make. It should be starting just in front of where the ball was. If it begins too far behind where the ball was, you are digging too soon. If the divot goes left or right, you are swinging too far inside or outside.*

HOLE 4

I f you want a personalized logo golf ball without ordering dozens of balls, then get the Golf Ball & Golf Tee Printer.

For about $25 you can buy "a true printing machine and not a toy." However, you won't be able to print your balls or tees immediately. You first must fill out a card with the name you want to imprint, send it to the company and wait for your one free printing plate. You can select block or script lettering and from 7-11 characters, depending on the type size. Additional plates are just $4.95 each and can be ordered at any time. You also can choose from dozens of stock logos of golf scenes

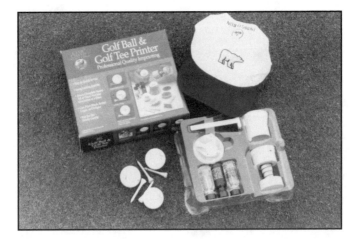

for $6.95 or get a custom logo made for just $10.

Once you have the printing plate, you are in business. It only takes a minute to print a ball, but it takes about five minutes for the ink to dry and another 10 minutes for the sealer to dry.

The original pack includes only one bottle of black ink and the sealer (enough to do about 200 balls), but you can order red, blue or green ink for just $2.95 per bottle.

The Golf Ball & Golf Tee Printer is made by Dennco Good Sports, Salem, New Hampshire, (603) 898-0004.

Jeff: What an imbecile you are! That shot you just hit struck me in the eye! I'm pursuing legal remedy to the tune of $7 million!

Randy: I believe I yelled, "Fore!"

Jeff: Oh, what the hell, I'll take it.

. . . .

Two guys at a convention get totally drunk the night before a big golf match.

During the match the two half-bombed characters manage to stay even with their opponents through 17 holes. On the 18th, by some miracle, they are in a position to win the match if one of them can sink his seven-foot putt.

The man sets up to putt with his feet wide apart. He draws his putter back. Just then a big black dog, chasing a squirrel, comes running across the green, the dog goes right between the guy's legs, and out the other side and runs off the green.

The guy never flinches but strokes the ball into the hole for the win!

His partner goes wild, shouting, "I have never seen

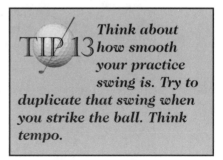

Think about how smooth your practice swing is. Try to duplicate that swing when you strike the ball. Think tempo.

such total concentration. How you managed to drop that putt with that dog running between your legs ..."

"Oh," says his partner, "Was that a real dog?"

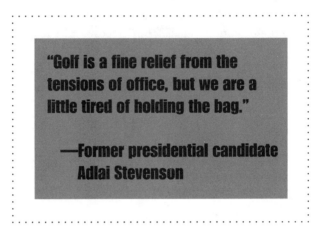

"Golf is a fine relief from the tensions of office, but we are a little tired of holding the bag."

—Former presidential candidate Adlai Stevenson

I f you just want to mark your balls the old-fashioned way, then consider the Dri Mark Golf Ball Marking Pen.

For just $2, you get two markers (one black and one red) loaded with permanent ink that stays on in wet or dry conditions. The ink dries quickly and survives multiple rounds. The pens fit easily into any golf bag pocket.

Follow the rules and mark your balls.

Dri Mark Golf Ball Marking Pens are made by Dri Mark Products, Inc. of Port Washington, New York, (516) 484-6200.

*M*anager: I'm sorry, sir. We have no time open on the course today.

Golfer: Wait a minute, what if Arnold Palmer and Jack Nicklaus showed up? I'm sure you'd find a starting time for them.

Manager: Of course we would, sir.

Golfer: Well, I happen to know they're not coming, so we'll take their time.

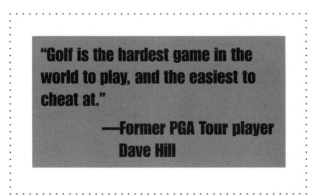

> **"Golf is the hardest game in the world to play, and the easiest to cheat at."**
>
> **—Former PGA Tour player Dave Hill**

A golfer goes into the pro shop and looks around frowning. Finally the pro asks him what he wants.

"I can't find any green golf balls," the golfer replies.

The pro looks all over the shop, and through all the catalogs, and finally calls the manufacturers and determines that sure enough, there are no green golf balls.

As the golfer walks out the door in disgust, the pro asks him, "Before you go, could you tell me why you want green golf balls?"

He replies, "Well, it's obvious! They would be so much easier to find in the sand traps!"

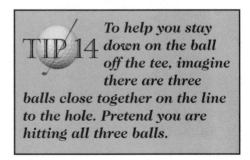

TIP 14 To help you stay down on the ball off the tee, imagine there are three balls close together on the line to the hole. Pretend you are hitting all three balls.

Use the latest laser technology to improve your golf swing. Plane Sight is a small laser device which easily attaches to almost any golf club. The laser light will show you where the butt of the club is pointing. It is a training device which can be used with your own club. As you swing the club, you will see a red laser line. You will see three distinct lines, one during your back swing, one during your down swing and one during your follow through. You can make adjustments to your swing plane based on your immediate feedback.

The package includes an instructional video and sells for $100. Call (800) 626-8924.

*O*ne day a prospective member went to an exclusive golf club and wanted to play the course before deciding to join. He inquired about the services of a caddie, but the clubhouse manager told him there were none available. The manager did say there were three robotic caddies.

The robots, the manager explained, would follow a golfer around the course, that they were trained to carry clubs and other necessities. He said the robots would also follow your shot, locate the ball and enter your score. These machines, the manager said, also would offer suggestions as to which club would be best for your next shot and would indicate potential obstacles to a successful shot.

The golfer said he'd give the robot a try. Off they went, returning a few hours later. The golfer beamed and exclaimed that he had just shot an all-time best round.

After thinking about the experience, he came back the next day, paid his fees and dues and became a club member. He also decided it would be best to set his tee time for Saturday.

Saturday came, and the golfer asked for the same robotic caddie. The manager said they were out of service. The manager said that the day after the golfer played his "life" round, the sun's rays beamed down on the reflective surface of the robot and zapped a bus driver in the eyes. Well, the bus careened off the road and several passengers were injured. When that happened, the manager said, he decided to retire the robots.

The newest member of the club suggested the manager attire the robots in some of the clothes in the lost-and-found locker.

The manager said that was tried. He said one of the robots believed he was Payne Stewart and refused to lug clubs and necessities unless the player was wearing plus-fours. Another robot believed he was the embodiment of Fuzzy Zoeller; he simply wanted to talk about his golf exploits. The third one, who believed he was Greg Norman kept humming the overture from "Jaws" and couldn't free himself from the pond off to the left of No. 9.

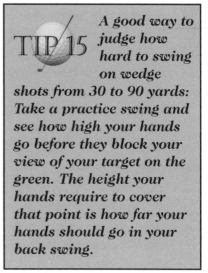

TIP 15 **A good way to judge how hard to swing on wedge shots from 30 to 90 yards: Take a practice swing and see how high your hands go before they block your view of your target on the green. The height your hands require to cover that point is how far your hands should go in your back swing.**

f you enjoy hunting for golf balls, but don't want to carry a long ball retriever, then consider an I GOTCHA. It collapses to just 14 inches, but has a telescoping shaft that extends up to 10 feet.

According to the package, "It took two and a half years to develop this effective, high-quality product."

It employs a spring-loaded polycarbonate head, metal telescopic shaft and solid rubber handle. It retails for about $35.

I GOTCHA is made by Pro Line Retrievers, Inc. in Lake Mary, Florida, (407) 805-0101.

*O*ne day a man went golfing. On the fourth tee he was separated from his friends momentarily, and bumped into a passing demon.

"Hey," said the demon, "how'd you like to make this one a hole-in-one?"

"What's the catch?" said the man suspiciously.

"It shortens your sex life by five years," replied the demon.

"Hmmm . . . OK," said the man, and went on to make a spectacular shot, a hole-in-one, just as ordered.

On the next tee, he again bumped into the demon.

"How'd you like to make it two holes-in-one consecutively?" said the demon. "It's only been done five times in the history of golf."

"What's the payback this time?" said the man.

"Shortens your sex life by another twenty years," said the demon.

"I guess," agreed the man, and again he made an amazing shot.

All his friends were amazed and people were coming from miles around to see him play. Just think, two holes-in-one in the same game!

On the next hole, the man again bumped into the demon, who proposed yet again. "Look, another hole-in-one would mean three in a row. It's never been done in the history of the world! C'mon!"

"No problem," said the man, agreeing. "What do I gotta give up this time?"

"You may never touch a person of the opposite sex ever again for the rest of your life," said the demon.

"OK!" said the man, and again he hit a hole-in-one.

And that's how Father Hoolihan got into the Guinness Book of Records!

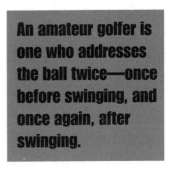

An amateur golfer is one who addresses the ball twice—once before swinging, and once again, after swinging.

*A*n ardent golfer dies and finds himself at the pearly gates.
St. Peter tells the man he has lived an exemplary life and that he can go right in.

The man asks, "St. Peter, where is the golf course?"

"I'm terribly sorry," replies St. Peter, "but that's one thing we don't have here."

The man turns and decides that he will see if the situation is any better in hell.

On the road to hell, he is greeted by the devil who has already heard of the golfer's rejection of heaven.

"This way, sir," says the devil, "to the finest tournament-quality 18 holes you are likely to find this side of Augusta, Georgia."

The golfer looks around and agrees that it is the finest course he has ever seen and decides he'd rather spend eternity there than in heaven, so he signs up for the full package.

"So," he says to the devil, "why don't you go get me some clubs and balls and I'll have the game of my after-life."

"I'm sorry, sir, we don't have any."

"What?" says the man. "No balls or clubs for a fine course like this?"

"No, sir," says the devil fiendishly, "that's the hell of it."

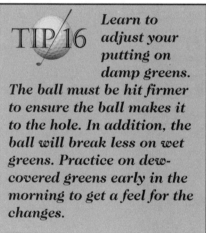

TIP 16 *Learn to adjust your putting on damp greens. The ball must be hit firmer to ensure the ball makes it to the hole. In addition, the ball will break less on wet greens. Practice on dew-covered greens early in the morning to get a feel for the changes.*

If you don't want to mess with carrying a retriever, then carry a Floating Golf Ball.

That's right—a golf ball that looks and feels like a regulation ball. The only difference is that it floats when it is hit into water. Save the cost of a lost water ball—in money and in strokes (assuming you are playing for fun).

The Floating Golf Ball is made by 19th Hole Brand Golf Products and distributed by Golf Gifts & Gallery, Inc.

A golfer, playing a round by himself, is about to tee off, and a greasy little salesman runs up to him, and yells, "Wait! Before you tee off, I have something really amazing to show you!"

The golfer, annoyed, says, "What is it?"

"It's a special golf ball," says the salesman. "You can never lose it!"

"Whattaya mean," scoffs the golfer, "you can never lose it? What if you hit it into the water?"

"No problem," says the salesman. "It floats, and it detects where the shore is, and spins towards it."

"Well, what if you hit it into the woods?"

"Easy," says the salesman. "It emits a beeping sound, and you can find it with your eyes closed."

"OK," says the golfer, impressed. "But what if your round goes late and it gets dark?"

"No problem, sir, this golf ball glows in the dark! I'm telling you, you can never lose this golf ball!"

The golfer buys it at once.

"Just one question," he says to the salesman. "Where did you get it?"

"I found it."

· · · · · · · · · · · · ·

Q: What should you do if your round of golf is interrupted by a lightning storm?

A: Walk around holding your 1-iron above your head, because even God can't hit a 1-iron.

What's The Whippy TempoMaster? It was invented by Dr. John N. Melvin for his own personal use. The TempoMaster has a double flex point shaft with the most noticeable flex point four inches below the hands with the second flex point being in the handle which lies under the pointer finger and should never be felt.

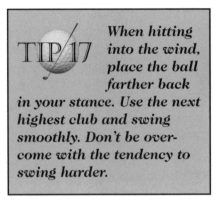

When hitting into the wind, place the ball farther back in your stance. Use the next highest club and swing smoothly. Don't be overcome with the tendency to swing harder.

The super flexible club is the closest you ever will get to hitting golf balls with something that has the same characteristics of a rock on a string. By using the TempoMaster, you will learn to generate club head speed using centrifugal force.

The Whippy comes in all sizes and lofts of clubs. They range in price from $99 (irons) to $119 (woods). The Whippy TempoMaster Co., Inc. is based in Dallas and can be reached at (800) 494-4779.

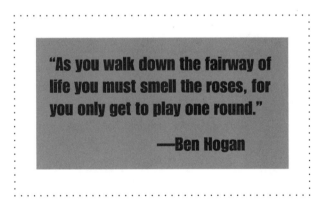

"As you walk down the fairway of life you must smell the roses, for you only get to play one round."

—Ben Hogan

*T*wo guys are driving around with their dogs in the back when they pass a new golf course.

"Hey, let's play that new course," says one of the guys. "I have two sets of clubs in the trunk, but what do we do with the dogs? We can't leave them in the car all day."

TIP/18 Make certain you are standing with your eyes directly over the ball when putting. How do you test that? Take your normal stance, then put a coin between your eyes and drop it. If it hits the ball, your head is in the proper position. If it doesn't, then adjust your stance accordingly. Test often. It isn't hard for poor habits to sneak into a weekend player's game.

One guy has a Doberman Pinscher and the other one has a Chihuahua. The guy with the Doberman Pinscher says to the guy with a Chihuahua, "Let's grab the dogs and go over to the starter and see if we can play."

The guy with the Chihuahua says, "We can't take the dogs. Look at that sign, "NO PETS ALLOWED!"

The guy with the Doberman Pinscher says, "Just follow my lead."

They walk over to the starter, the guy with the Doberman Pinscher puts on a pair of dark glasses, and he starts to walks to the first tee.

The starter says, "Sorry, Mac, no pets allowed."

The guy with the Doberman Pinscher says, "You don't understand. I have very poor eyesight and this is my seeing-eye dog."

The starter says, "A Doberman Pinscher?"

He says, "Yes, they're using them now, they're very good."

The starter says, "Hit away and have a nice round."

The guy with the Chihuahua figures, What the hell, so he puts on a pair of dark glasses and walks to the first tee.

The starter says, "Sorry, pal, no pets allowed."

The guy with the Chihuahua says, "You don't understand. I have very poor eyesight and this is my seeing-eye dog."

The guy at the door says, "A Chihuahua?"

The guy with the Chihuahua says, "You mean they gave me a Chihuahua?"

HOLE 5

The Anderson Line is a putting training device that can be used indoors or out. It is a metal bar connected by two inverted "Vs" that helps you take your putter straight back and straight through.

It also trains your eyes to accurately read the actual target line and helps you position your body parallel to the correct line.

Constructed of galvanized metal and black powder-baked for a non-glare finish, it includes rubber tips for non-slip stability on any surface. It comes with a metal "hole" and disassembles to fit into most golf bags.

The Anderson Line is a product of The GAMB Corp. in Chicago and sells for $49.95. Call (888) 863-5599.

TIP 19

If you want to see your scores improve, spend time on the practice range. Loosen up by hitting balls before every round, then return to the range after a round to work on certain aspects of your game. Do not use the course to make major changes in your swing. During your round, enjoy your time on the course. Save the work for afterward.

A hack golfer spends a day at a plush country club, playing golf,
enjoying the luxury of a complimentary caddie.

Being a hack golfer, he plays poorly all day.

At the 18th hole, he spots a lake to the left of the fairway. He
looks at the caddie and says, "I've played so poorly all day, I think I'm
going to go drown myself in that lake."

The caddie looks back at him and says, "I don't think you could
keep your head down that long."

A golfer ran into an
old buddy at the
driving range one day.

They talked about
their games, their
swings, and all manner
of things.

Eventually, one of
them said, "How's the
family?"

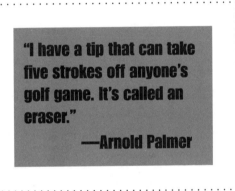

"I have a tip that can take
five strokes off anyone's
golf game. It's called an
eraser."

—Arnold Palmer

The other replied, "Oh, pretty good. I got a new set of clubs for
the wife the other day!"

"Hey, good trade!" replied the former good buddy.

N o room in your golf bag for complete rain gear? Then get a
pack of Disposaballs.

This clever little package provides all the necessary rain gear in
three golf ball-sized packages. One "ball" contains a scorecard cover, one
a club cover and another is a gear bag that allows you to protect your
cell phone, street shoes and extra clothing.

Each "sleeve" of Disposaballs is just $9.95 and is available through
Denali Products, Inc. of Jenison, Michigan, (800) 955-6221.

*T*hree very religious rabbis in black with long beards were playing golf.

A guy named Mulhaney wanted to play golf and this was the only threesome in which he could play. So he joins the rabbis and plays 18 holes.

At the end of the game his score is 104. The rabbis shot 69, 70 and 71.

He says to them, "How come you all play such good golf?"

The lead rabbi said, "When you live a religious life, join and attend temple, you are rewarded."

Mulhaney loves golf and figures, What do I have to lose?

So he finds a temple close to his home, attends twice a week, converts, joins and lives a holy life.

About a year later he again plays golf with the three rabbis. He shoots a 104 and they shoot 69, 70, 71.

He says to them, "OK, I joined a temple, live a religious life and I'm still shooting lousy."

The lead rabbi said to him, "What temple did you join?"

He said, "Beth Shalom."

The rabbi retorted, "Schmuck! That one's for tennis!"

TIP 20 Think of golf as a chess game. Think two or three moves ahead. Before you tee off, think of where you want to be on the green. Then think of where your approach shot needs to be played from to reach that point on the green. Then consider how to get to that approach area from the tee. Don't be afraid to use a 3-wood or iron off the tee if you stand a better chance of winding up in that approach area.

Why are golf and sex so similar?
They are the two things you can thoroughly enjoy even though you are really bad at them.

Denali Products, Inc. also offers a number of other unique items:

Clubtub is a plastic water-and-detergent club cleaner that stores easily in any garage or on any patio. Polypropylene brushes whisk away dirt on both sides of the club while a bottom brush cleans the sole of the club. A heavy duty non-marring gasket keeps you from getting splashed. The device cleans both irons and fairway woods. It costs $39.95.

Caddie-Mate is a unique golf club holder that carries up to four clubs and sticks into the ground to provide temporary support for clubs that are not in use. It eliminates wet grips and fertilizer covered shafts. It even has a towel ring. It sells for $19.95.

Iron Gloves are covers that protect the heads of your clubs. They are constructed of neoprene, with double-threaded stitching and reinforced endpoints. The Iron Glove goes on and off the club head without the hassle of hard rubber covers and it fits into your pocket while you hit a shot. Available in three different colors, Iron Gloves cost $19.95 for a set of eight covers.

Joey Coolers allow you to keep your drinks cold without worrying about ice. They are made of nylon insulating material and each has its own cooler pack that you simply keep in the freezer until you are ready to use it. The cooler pack cradles each can in place while the pouch surrounds the entire unit. It comes in red or black, three-($16.75) or six-can size ($25.95).

Virtual Turf is the most realistic practice hitting mat available. It is designed to simulate striking a golf ball from natural grass while providing durability. The single filament, wound composite material is formed into a "leaf spring" that serves as the actual hitting surface. Artificial turf is applied to the spring with special adhesive, giving you a hitting surface that "gives" just as if you were taking a real divot from the fairway. It sells for $425.

All of these items are available by calling (800) 955-6221.

A golfer is walking through the club lot one day when another walks up carrying the finest clubs available.

"Where did you get THOSE?" asked the first.

The second replied, "Well, I was walking along yesterday minding my own business, when a beautiful woman came up to me. She threw her husband's new clubs to the ground, took off all her clothes and said, 'Take what you want.'"

TIP 21 To make more putts, concentrate on the distance, rather than the direction. Determine the proper direction the putt needs to roll, pick out a target, align your body and putter blade. If you make a straight, consistent stroke, the ball will head in the direction you want. Think distance.

The first man nodded with approval. "Good choice. The clothes probably wouldn't have fit."

*M*ake putting on your home or office carpet more realistic with Sink-A-Putt.

It gives you the real feel of a putt dropping into the cup. There are no ramps or obstacles because it fits into the floor. It lays flush with the top of the carpet, thereby providing a level putting surface.

It can be used in up to 90 percent of homes with floor registers because of its multiple size range. It fits any register with dimensions of 4 to 5 and-a-half inches by 10 to 15 and-a-half inches.

It installs in seconds with no tools. Simply lift out the floor register and drop Sink-A-Putt into place. It comes with a handy flag stick that doubles as a ball remover and a way to open or close off the air flow from your heater. It retails for about $20.

*A*n American tourist was playing golf at Waterville County, Kerry in Ireland, where he came to a hole with a fast-flowing river running down the side of the fairway.

A young boy was sitting at the bank of the river. The tourist hooked his drive and hit the boy who fell into the river.

By the time the worried golfer arrived at the river bank, the boy was sinking into the deep water for the third time and was looking poorly. The tourist immediately jumped into the river and after a real struggle managed to bring the boy to dry land where he quickly revived him. He then brought the boy back to the clubhouse where he arranged for a taxi to take the boy home.

About an hour later a man arrived at the clubhouse and asked the pro, "Could you tell me where the man is who saved my son?"

The pro replied, "He's over in the hotel. Check with the receptionist."

The man then went to the hotel and asked the receptionist, "Could you tell me where the man is who saved my son?"

"Yes, I'll call his room and ask him to come down," was the reply.

A few minutes later the American tourist came down.

The man asked him, "Are you the man who saved my son?"

"Yes, I sure am," was the reply.

"Well, would you have his cap?"

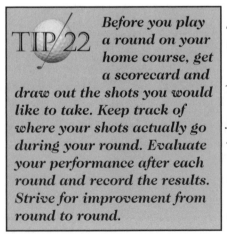

TIP 22 Before you play a round on your home course, get a scorecard and draw out the shots you would like to take. Keep track of where your shots actually go during your round. Evaluate your performance after each round and record the results. Strive for improvement from round to round.

To use a more realistic putting surface than your carpet, get a DreamGreen.

DreamGreen brings what indoor golf has always needed: realism. The product features a selectively contourable putting surface that resembles a freshly mowed green. There are tens of thousands of possible combinations of contours, right or left breaks, combination breaks, uphill and downhill, as well as from various distances.

Made of solid cherry, walnut or teak wood, the DreamGreen standard surfaces come in widths of 2 to 4 feet and lengths of 8 to 12 feet. They range in price from $599 to $2,695. Custom surfaces also are available.

The DreamGreen is made by Duffy Golf Inc. and available by calling Golf Traditions at (812) 443-4653.

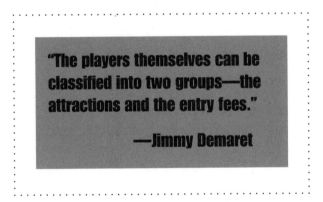

"The players themselves can be classified into two groups—the attractions and the entry fees."

—Jimmy Demaret

There were three pieces of string sitting across the street from an exclusive golf club, wishing to play.

The first string gathered enough courage to enter the clubhouse and approach the pro. "How much to play nine holes?" the string asked. The pro pointed towards the door, "Out," he said, "We don't allow strings on the golf course." The string went back to his friends and told them what had occurred.

The second string gathered his wits and charged into the clubhouse, "I'm playing golf today. My money's good, so issue me a cart and I'll be off." "Out!" Shouted the pro. "We don't allow strings here. It's a semi-private club and the members have made it clear. No strings." The string returned and explained all that had transpired.

The third string, being the smartest of the three, tied himself into a knot. "Now," he said, "shred my ends." His friends did as he asked and he bounced into the clubhouse. "I'm playing eighteen today," he announced.

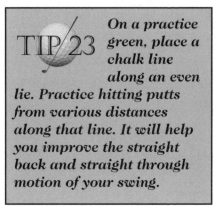

TIP 23 On a practice green, place a chalk line along an even lie. Practice hitting putts from various distances along that line. It will help you improve the straight back and straight through motion of your swing.

The pro glared at him a moment and issued a cart. As the string handed him a credit card, the pro asked: "Are you a string by chance?" "No, I'm a frayed knot!"

A golfer is playing a round with his buddies. The sixth hole requires a tee shot to carry over a large lake. He proceeds to flub nine balls into the water. Frustrated over his poor golfing ability, and about ready to hit somebody, he heaves his golf clubs into the water, and begins to walk off the course.

Then all of a sudden he turns around and jumps into the lake, his buddies apparently thinking he is going to retrieve his clubs.

When he comes out of the water he doesn't have his clubs and begins to walk off the course. Then one of his buddies asks, "Why did you jump into the lake?"

"I left my car keys in the bag."

Hank Bickler has created training devices to help with chipping and putting. After observing golfers for more than 20 years, he came up with the Bickler Chipping Trainer (about $20) and Bickler Putting Trainer (about $20).

Both are endorsed by Ken Venturi and John Cook and both devices emphasize the proper angle between the forearms and the club shaft. A correct angle assures the face of the club or putter being square to the ball at impact.

The sturdy metal braces are easy to attach to the clubs and are strong enough to keep anyone's forearm in place. The "V" created by your wrists keeps your arms in the proper place throughout the stroke.

Bickler trainers are distributed by La Jolla Club Golf Company in Vista, California, (619) 599-9400.

A golfer hit his drive on the first hole 300 yards right down the middle. When it came down, however, it hit a sprinkler and the ball went sideways into the woods. He was angry, but he went into the woods and hit a very hard 2 iron which hit a tree

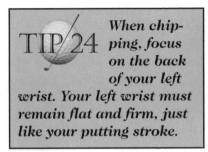

TIP 24 When chipping, focus on the back of your left wrist. Your left wrist must remain flat and firm, just like your putting stroke.

and bounced back straight at him. It hit him in the temple and killed him.

He was at the Pearly Gates and St. Peter looked at the big book and said, "I see you were a golfer. Is that correct?"

"Yes, I am," he replied.

St. Peter said, "Do you hit the ball a long way?"

The golfer replied, "You bet. After all, I got here in two, didn't I?"

· · · · · · · · · · · ·

T wo golfers were sitting at the 19th hole discussing their games when one says to the other, "My game is so bad this year, I had to have my ball retriever regripped!"

I f you often lose count of your strokes on a hole, then get one of JP Lann Golf's inexpensive score keepers.

For just $3 you can get a Wrist Score Keeper that resembles a watch. Just spin the dials to keep track of your score on a hole, as well as your round.

For just $2.50, you can get a Bead Counter. The counter uses plastic golf ball beads on a nylon braid. It clips to a golf bag or belt. However, hackers beware. There are only 10 beads, so no scores over 10.

JP Lann Golf of Royal Oak, Michigan, distributes its products by Nefouse Enterprises, Inc. For more information, call (248) 549-5554.

TIP 25

Watch as much golf on TV as you can. What better swing is there to emulate than the swing of a professional player? Observe the set-up and rhythm. Do not pay attention to their club selection, except around the green. Just because Greg Norman hits an 8-iron 165 yards does not mean that's how far you should hit an 8-iron. But do pay attention to the use of clubs for chips and pitches. There's a reason why those golfers are on TV. They are the best at what they do.

The golfer called one of the caddies and said, "I want a caddie who can count and keep the score. What's 3 and 4 and 5 add up to?"

"Eleven, sir," said the caddie.

"Good, you'll do perfectly."

Joe decides to take his boss, Phil, to play 9 holes on their lunch hour. While both men are playing excellent they are often held up by two women in front of them moving at a very slow pace.

Joe offers to talk to the women and see if they can speed it up a bit. He gets about three-quarters of the way, stops and jogs back. His boss asks what the problem is.

Joe said, "Well one of those women is my wife and the other my mistress. Phil just shook his head at Joe and started towards the women determined to finish his round of golf.

Preparing to ask the ladies to hurry their game, he too stopped short and turned around. Joe asked, "What's wrong?"

"It's a small, small world Joe, and you're fired."

What to do about that crumpled golf glove between rounds? Use a Golf Glove Keeper.

The plastic pliable mold, shaped like a hand, will keep any sports glove in the proper form between uses. It also can be used to help dry a sweaty or wet glove. Good for right or left handed gloves. The mold can clip onto a golf bag or be tossed into a bag pocket. It sells for about $2.50 and is made by On Course.

Pete and Gladys were looking to join the exclusive new country club in the neighborhood.

Pete says to the general manager, "We really like it here, but I don't think we can afford it."

The general manager says, "You just make a small down payment, then you don't make another payment for six months."

Gladys turns around with her hands on her hips and says, "Who told you about us?"

A priest is playing a round of golf at the local public course when he arrives at the 14th tee. It is a 160-yard, par-3 with a lake in the front of the green. It is also the padre's nemesis, no matter how well or how poorly he is playing.

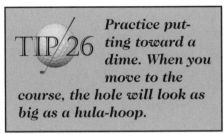

TIP/26 *Practice putting toward a dime. When you move to the course, the hole will look as big as a hula-hoop.*

Upon arriving at the tee, the priest tees up his ball, gets ready to hit and, at the last minute, looks toward the heavens and says, "God, I have been a good and decent man. Please, just this once, let me hit a shot which will carry the lake and get onto the green."

As he is about to swing, a loud, deep voice booms from the heavens and says, "Use a new ball; they go farther."

The priest steps back, thinks about the heavenly advice and goes to his bag and gets a brand new ball.

He takes his stance and once again the heavenly voice booms, "Take a practice swing first."

The priest is now awestruck by the heavenly advice, so he steps back from the ball and takes a practice swing. He takes his stance and gets ready to hit and the heavenly voice booms, "Use the old ball."

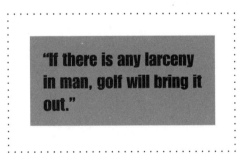

"If there is any larceny in man, golf will bring it out."

When baseball pitchers want to dry their hands, they reach for a rosin bag. When gymnasts want to prepare for a routine on the bars, they reach for the rosin. So, what do golfers do when they get sweaty hands from pressure situations or the heat?

Now golfers have the option of going to the rosin bag. The rosin makes hands tacky for a better grip. It stores easily in a resealable plastic bag and can be kept in your pants pocket or golf bag.

Powdered Rosin Bags (retail about $2) are made by Columbia 300, Inc. of San Antonio, Texas, (210) 344-9211.

W *hich is the easiest golf shot?*
The fourth putt.

· · · · · · · · · · · ·

A *man had been drivinga all night and by morning was still far from his destination. He decided to stop at the next city he came to, and park somewhere quiet so he could get an hour or two of sleep. As luck would have it, the quiet place he chose happened to be in the parking lot of a municipal golf course, right next to the driving range. No sooner had he settled back to snooze when there came a knocking on his window. He looked out and saw a golfer stretching with a club.*

"Yes?"

"Excuse me, sir," the golfer said, "do you have the time?"

The man looked at the car clock and answered, "7:15."

The golfer said thanks and left. The man settled

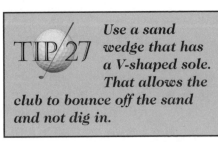

TIP/27 Use a sand wedge that has a V-shaped sole. That allows the club to bounce off the sand and not dig in.

back again, and was just dozing off when there was another knock on the window and another golfer.

"Excuse me, sir, do you have the time?"

"7:25!"

The golfer said thanks and left. Now the man could see other golfers passing by and he knew it was only a matter of time before another one disturbed him. To avoid the problem, he got out a pen and paper and put a sign in his window saying, "I do not know the time!"

Once again he settled back to sleep. He was just dozing off when there was another knock on the window.

"Sir? It's 7:45."

Another device used extensively in baseball is weighted donut that slides onto a bat. On-deck hitters swing the weighted bat in preparation of their at bat.

Swinging a weighted golf club has many benefits. It can

strengthen the muscles used in the swing. Used properly, it also can give a golfer the feel of the natural arc of a swing using centrifugal force.

On Course makes an 8-ounce donut-style weight for just $2.50.

The justice of the peace in a small town was about to tee off with two other friends one day when the club pro volunteered to join them.

It seemed like the perfect opportunity for a free lesson. But instead of being helpful the pro was openly critical of the JP's game. At every bumbled shot, the pro made a joke about the justice. But the criticism didn't even stop at the end of the round.

The pro continued to embarrass the JP in the clubhouse among his friends. Finally the pro got up to leave and said, "Judge, let's do it again sometime. If you can't find anybody else to make a foursome, I'll be glad to play with you again."

"Well that would be fine," the justice of the peace said. "How about next Saturday? I don't think any of my friends can join us, so why don't you just have your parents join us, and after our round I can marry them."

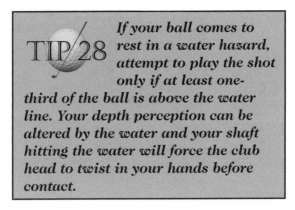

TIP 28 If your ball comes to rest in a water hazard, attempt to play the shot only if at least one-third of the ball is above the water line. Your depth perception can be altered by the water and your shaft hitting the water will force the club head to twist in your hands before contact.

HOLE 7

The Swing-eez is a simple training aid designed to improve your tempo and rhythm. At the risk of oversimplifying the device, it's a plastic ball attached to a regulation golf grip by a rubber cord. It's designed to help ingrain a rhythmic swing and to eliminate "hitting from the top" and other tempo-related swing flaws. In addition, it's lightweight and flexible so that it can be stored in your golf bag for a pre-round warm-up (or a desperate mid-round quick fix).

It's available for $39.95 (including a video) from Hutchins Golf Products of Brea, California, (800) 495-0333.

This is a true story. Nobody could make this up.

Several years ago a couple put on a class called "Golf For Novices."

It was for beginner golfers to teach them the very basics of the game. It included such things as the grip, stance and the swing. They also covered things like etiquette and what to expect when you make your first trip to a golf course.

They mentioned that at the course there are two colored tees. The men play the blue tees and the women play the red tees.

A few weeks later John arrived home fairly late one evening from his golf game. He was living with Susy, who happened to have been

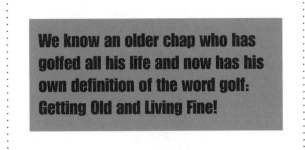

We know an older chap who has golfed all his life and now has his own definition of the word golf: Getting Old and Living Fine!

one of the enthusiastic, but not-too-bright, students.

She was somewhat agitated that he arrived home late but it wasn't until he emptied his pockets onto his dresser that she went ballistic. She flew into an intense rage and demanded to know who the woman was that he had been golfing with.

He hadn't a clue what her problem was and said he'd been playing with his pals, Brad, Jim and Elmer.

She continued her tirade and said, "Don't you lie to me. I know you were with some woman."

Finally he asked her to explain where she was coming from.

She replied, "I know you were with some woman because I took that beginners golfer course. They told me women play red tees and you just put some red tees on your dresser!"

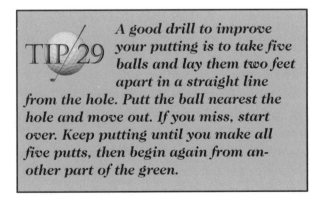

TIP/29 A good drill to improve your putting is to take five balls and lay them two feet apart in a straight line from the hole. Putt the ball nearest the hole and move out. If you miss, start over. Keep putting until you make all five putts, then begin again from another part of the green.

Don't get caught using a dirty ball off the tee. Any debris on a ball can cause changes in the rotation of the ball in flight. That means less than expected results. Don't run the risk that ball washers might not be available at every tee box. Carry your own washer with you.

For $59.95 you can get a Golf Clean washer that attaches to your golf cart. It's easy on and easy off, so you can take it with you, even when you rent carts. It also includes a club cleaner and comes in nine different colors, from Masters Green to Black. Call Golf Clean, Inc. at New Port Richey, Florida, (727) 841-6726..

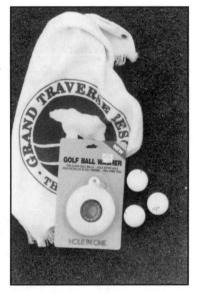

Or you can get a Hole In One Golf Ball Washer that attaches to your bag for just $8. Shaped like a donut, the Washer has a plastic shell surrounding a soft sponge. Just add water to the detergent-impregnated sponge at the start of a round. When your ball gets dirty, simply insert the ball and rotate it in the center of the hole.

Hole In One Inc. is based in Toronto, Canada.

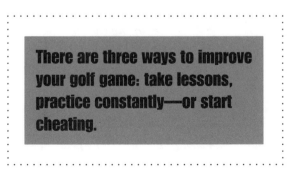

There are three ways to improve your golf game: take lessons, practice constantly—or start cheating.

*P*ete and Ray are playing one day. On the first hole, Pete hits a wicked slice into the adjoining fairway. The ball hits another player right between the eyes and he drops to the ground.

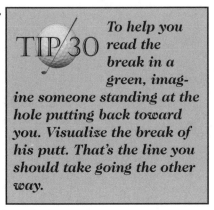

To help you read the break in a green, imag-ine someone standing at the hole putting back toward you. Visualize the break of his putt. That's the line you should take going the other way.

Pete and Ray rush over to the prostrate man and find him unconscious with the ball laying on the ground between his legs.

Pete screams, "Oh, my God, what should I do?"

Ray replies; "Don't move him. If you leave him there he becomes an immovable obstruction and, according to the rules, you are allowed a drop two club lengths away."

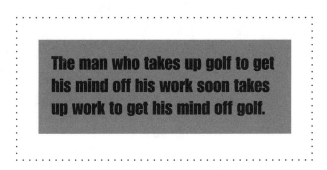

The man who takes up golf to get his mind off his work soon takes up work to get his mind off golf.

*J*im and Bob were golfing one fine day, when Jim, an avid golfer, slices his ball deep into a wooded ravine.

Jim takes his 8 iron and proceeds down the embankment into the ravine, in search of his lost ball. The brush is quite thick, but Jim searches diligently for his errant ball. Suddenly Jim spots something shiny. As he nears the location of the shiny object, Jim realizes that it is an 8 iron in the hands of a skeleton laying near an old golf ball.

Jim excitedly calls for his partner Bob. "Hey Bob, come here, I got trouble down here." Bob comes running over to the edge of the ravine and calls out to Jim, "What's the matter, Jim?"

Jim shouts back in a nervous voice, "Bring me my 7 iron. You can't get out of here with an 8."

One of the most popular aids on the market is the Amazing Assist Swing Trainer. More than 300,000 have been sold world-wide. It has a bright yellow hollowed club head, a crooked shaft and a grip that conforms to your hands. So, how does all of that help?

Its precision bent shaft exaggerates the release to teach the correct hand action for longer, straighter shots. Whether you are at home, in the office or at the range, swinging the Amazing Assist a few minutes each day makes practice easy. It's ideal for pre-game or pre-practice warm-up. The Amazing Assist is available for right- and left-handed players, and comes in different weights for men, women and juniors.

The cost is $75 from Matzie Golf Co., Inc. of Palm Desert, California, (888) 932-9700.

Matzie also makes the new Cast-Away Power Angle Trainer. It sells for $125. The training aid looks and feels like a normal iron. However, the bottom third of the shaft is connected with a hinge device that allows the club head to dangle freely.

Take a swing with the club. When you are at the top of your back swing, your wrists are fully cocked and the Cast-Away club head is hanging down. As the down swing begins, the shaft still is angled. It remains bent until the shaft straightens just prior to the point of impact. Any movement other than perfect timing and tempo will result in the shaft being angled through the impact area.

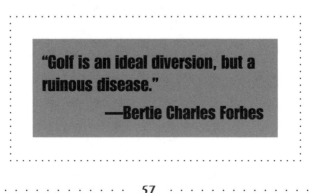

"Golf is an ideal diversion, but a ruinous disease."

—Bertie Charles Forbes

*A*bout four or five years ago I was standing in a ticket line at LAX, and a fellow in a line parallel to mine had a golf bag slung over his shoulder. Since the line was long and airline ticketing is a slow process at best, we struck up a conversa-

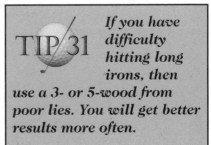

TIP 31 *If you have difficulty hitting long irons, then use a 3- or 5-wood from poor lies. You will get better results more often.*

tion. He brightened when I admired his golf bag, and he proudly stated that he was on the PGA Tour. Then he turned to me and asked the question all golfers ask: "Do you play?"

I shook my head. "I used to, but I quit because I wasn't good. I shot consistently in the lower seventies."

There was a long, low in-take of breath, then, "The lower seventies?"

"Yes," I admitted.

Consistently?" he queried admiringly.

"Every hole," I confessed.

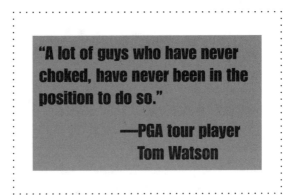

"A lot of guys who have never choked, have never been in the position to do so."

—PGA tour player
Tom Watson

A man and his gorilla are sitting in the clubhouse when the club champion comes in.

"I'll bet you $500 per hole my gorilla can play better golf than you," says the man.

The champion looks at the man, looks at the gorilla, and says, "You're on."

And off they go to the first tee. The first hole is a long par-4 over water. The man gives the champion the honors.

The champion tees up and hits a beautiful drive straight up the middle, over the water, chipping distance from the green.

> **TIP/32** Whenever you are playing from the rough, open your club face a bit. The longer the rough, the more you should open the club face. Why? The grass will catch the hosel of the club and twist the club face just prior to impact.

"Nice shot," says the man.

The gorilla then tees up, booms the drive onto the green, and into the hole!

The champ picks up his ball and they head off to the next hole, a beautiful par-five along the creek with a slight dog-leg left. The gorilla tees up and booms another drive, drawing it just enough to land it on the green, inches from the pin.

The champ, humiliated, concedes the hole and the match.

They head back to the clubhouse. As they settle the bet, the champ remarks how well the gorilla plays.

"I've never seen anyone drive it as far. By the way, since he aced the first hole and I conceded the match before finishing the second, I never got to see how he putts."

"Oh," says the man, pocketing his money, "he putts just exactly like he drives!"

*A*t the club's annual board meeting, the president was just about to finish, when one of the members stopped him:

"There is one more item to discuss, the exclusion of Mr. Petersen."

"Why?" asked the president.

"Last week he jumped our new secretary in the bunker at hole 9."

"So, we all would like to do that. It is not a reason for exclusion!"

"Yes, but he did not rake the bunker afterward, damnit!"

If you own your own cart, there are a variety of add-ons available. Powell's Equipment Service, Inc. in Ft. Bragg, North Carolina, offers a number of golf car accessories.

For $18 you can get an EZGO backrest cover. For $36 you get a seat cover. For $30 you get a battery voltage indicator. For $24 get a five-panel mirror. And to liven up your wheels, get a chrome cover for $8 each, black and gold covers for $8 each or wire chrome covers for $15 each.

If you want your golf car to be used for more than just golf, you can add utility beds or boxes to the back. A 40 x 24 x 10-inch box is $160; a 45 x 32 x 9-inch bed is $240.

Call (910) 424-6737 to purchase your cart accessories.

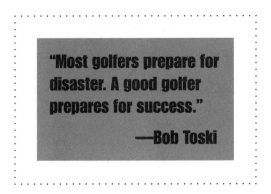

"Most golfers prepare for disaster. A good golfer prepares for success."

—Bob Toski

*A*fter an enjoyable eighteen holes of golf, a man stopped in a bar for a beer before heading home.

There he struck up a conversation with a ravishing young beauty. They had a couple of drinks, liked each other, and soon she invited him over to her apartment.

For two hours they made mad, passionate love.

On the way home, the man's conscience started bothering him something awful. He loved his wife and didn't want this unplanned indiscretion to ruin their relationship, so he decided the only thing to do was come clean.

"Honey," he said when he got home, *"I have a confession to make. After I played golf today, I stopped by the bar for a beer, met a beautiful woman, went back to her apartment and made love to her for two hours. I'm sorry, it won't ever happen again, and I hope you'll forgive me."*

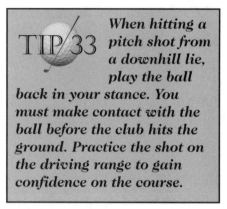

When hitting a pitch shot from a downhill lie, play the ball back in your stance. You must make contact with the ball before the club hits the ground. Practice the shot on the driving range to gain confidence on the course.

His wife scowled at him and said, "Don't lie to me, you sorry scum bag! You played thirty-six holes, didn't you?"

f you are still looking for more options for your own cart, then contact The Golf Car Catalog at (800) 328-1953. Consider these add-ons:

Grab Handle (to assist you getting out of the cart). ($6.95)
Cooler Bag. ($28.00)
Lockable Dash Tray. ($84.95)
Smoothie Rake with Holder. ($24.95)
Chrome Tee Dispenser. ($14.95)
"Please Keep Feet Off" Decal. ($1.75)
Medical Identification Flag. ($7.95)
Bottle Top Heater. ($30.95)
Steering Wheel Knob. ($19.95)
Cup Holder Tray. ($12.00)
Seat Belts. ($23.10 each)
Side Saddle Baskets. ($37.95)

*T*om once played a course that was so tough, he lost three balls in the ball washer!

· · · · · · · · · · · ·

*O*ne day Jesus, Moses, and some old guy were playing golf. Jesus teed off and it landed in the water, so he walked on the water to retrieve the ball.

Moses was next, he hit the ball into the water so he parted the water and got his ball.

Then the old man teed off; the ball was heading for the water too when a fish swallowed the ball.

But before the fish returned into the water a heron grabbed the fish and the heron flew over the green and the fish dropped the ball into the cup for an ace.

Then Moses turned to Jesus and said, "I hate playing with your father."

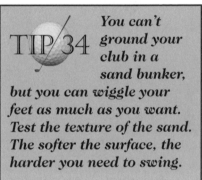

TIP 34 You can't ground your club in a sand bunker, but you can wiggle your feet as much as you want. Test the texture of the sand. The softer the surface, the harder you need to swing.

Sign posted in a locker room: LOST: Golfter husband and his trusty dog. Last seen at Fox Ranch Golf Links. Reward for dog.

HOLE 8

ny ball hit on the sweet spot of a club is going to fly straighter and farther than one that is hit off center. But how do you know for certain where you are making contact on the club face? Use an Accu-Master. It's presented by Butch Harmon, the coach for Tiger Woods.

The Accu-Master is a pad that attaches to virtually any club face via an adhesive backing. Hit a ball and a sensor lights at the point of impact. The light fades in about 20 seconds. Each pad, which sells for about $7, lasts for

about 150 hits in ideal conditions. Using it in extreme cold or hot temperatures can affect its life, as will taking deep divots.

The Accu-Master is distributed by Accu-Marketing of Salt Lake City, (801) 467-4004.

*A*n avid golfer dies and finds himself at the pearly gates. St. Peter greets him and tells him that he has a tee time at Heaven's replica course of Pebble Beach and that some of his old golfing friends are already at the tee waiting for him.

Furthermore, he has a starting time the next morning at the replica of St. Andrews and that he can check in after that for his future starting times.

He joins his old friends and has a fine day at Pebble Beach. His golf is not perfect (that would be hell) but he is striking the ball well, has back his old vigor, and is ready to go the next morning at St. Andrews.

When he checks in the next day, St. Peter inquires about his game and asks him if there is anything else that can be done to make his stay more enjoyable.

"Well, St. Peter," says the golfer, "This is fantastic. If it hadn't been for all that Oat Bran my wife had been feeding me, I could have been here seven years ago."

Find a putter you like and stick with it. If the course you normally play has fast greens, you'll do better with a light putter. If the greens are slow, then get a heavier putter. However, don't try to guess the speed and alter the club head's weight from round to round.

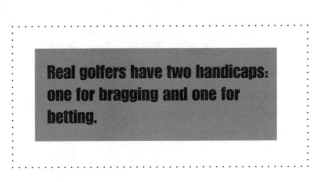

Real golfers have two handicaps: one for bragging and one for betting.

Have you ever bought a golf bag that won't hold all of your miscellaneous items such as balls, tees, gloves, umbrella, shoes, etc.? There never seem to be enough pockets to hold everything you need.

Then find a PicPocket Golf Bag. For the standard rate of $139, you literally can build your own golf bag. Do you want a pocket for balls on one side rather than the other? Two pockets, three, maybe four? You pick the side and quantity, too. Do you want a large pocket, rather than an average-sized pocket? Pick that, too. Do you want a water bottle pack, valuables pack or special cigar case? Just say so. Now, do you want a single or double carrying strap? How about color-coordinated head covers, too? Colors? You can mix or match practically any combination you want.

Contact PicPocket Golf of Vancouver, British Columbia, at (888) 862-2515.

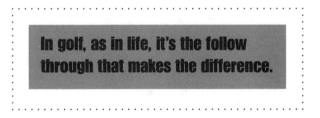

In golf, as in life, it's the follow through that makes the difference.

*P*oetic justice?
Your first golf shot of the day is never made to order.

Rarely down the middle, usually in the water.

Your second slices in the woods a place no man dare tread.

Your gutsy third comes whizzing back and almost takes your head.

When using an iron on par-3 holes, tee the ball. Experiment on the range with various heights, but normally tee the ball 1/4-inch above the ground for short irons and 1/2-inch for longer irons. By using a tee, you will strike the ball solidly more often.

You chip your fourth back into play.
Your fifth lands in the beach.
Your sixth sprays sand but it's still there,
Your seventh just might reach.
Oh well, two putts for nine, it happens now and then.
Oh, no! Your ninth just rimmed the cup. Oh, man, you took a ten!

What's in a name? A good slogan. Take The Bermuda Triangle Putter: "It makes your putts disappear!"

The putter has a patented triangle design where the club head meets the shaft. It's designed that way to keep the putter head square to the target. The higher center of gravity eliminates backspin and guarantees smooth rolls to the cup. And the largest sweet spot ever designed for a putter ensures total confidence on the green.

If all of that isn't enough, the putter is endorsed by Jamie Farr of M*A*S*H television fame.

The putter is available for $100 from Bermuda Triangle Golf, LLC, of Laguna Hills, California, (800) 466-9477.

A woman was talking to the other three members of her foursome about her husband had passed away.

When her husband was on his deathbed, he told her that he had three envelopes in his desk drawer that would "take care" of all of the arrangements. Well, he died shortly thereafter, so the wife opened the drawer and there were three envelopes just like he said.

On the first envelope it said, "for the casket." There was $5,000 in the envelope, so she bought him a very nice casket.

The second envelope said, "for the expenses" and had $4,000 in it so she paid all the bills from the funeral.

The third envelope said, "for the stone" and had $3,000 in it. She then held out her hand to her friends and said, "Isn't it beautiful!?!"

A grasshopper hops along the 18th fairway, then goes into the clubhouse bar and hops onto a barstool to order a drink.

The bartender says, "You know, we have a drink named after you?"

The grasshopper replies, "Really? You have a drink named Eddie?"

TIP 37 When you try to judge the wind, don't just throw a few blades of grass into the breeze. Look at the top of the trees. That's where your ball will (should) be traveling. Wind speed and direction can vary drastically between ground level and the tree tops.

G olfer: Would you mind wading into the pond and retrieving my ball?
Caddie: Why?
Golfer: It's my lucky ball.

S chooler Corporation of Clinton Township, Michigan, has a different twist on putter designs. Its Schooler Pro Touch Putter has a round head and an adjustable shaft.

The head is made from Delrin to give it durability and greater impact resistance. The round shape gives the ball smoother rolling ability when struck, with less skipping. The shaft adjusts through a 20-degree range to give you the correct lie. The adjustable angle and unique head allows the club to be used by either right- or left-handed players. Other features that make it easier

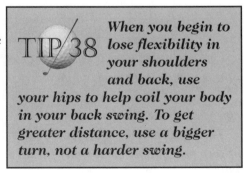

TIP 38 When you begin to lose flexibility in your shoulders and back, use your hips to help coil your body in your back swing. To get greater distance, use a bigger turn, not a harder swing.

to hit the sweet spot include the shaft connected to the center of the head and alignment lines that equal the diameter of a golf ball.

The putter costs $95. For more information, call (888) 282-CLUB.

*F*or most of the round the golfer had argued with his caddie about club selection, but the caddie always prevailed.

Finally, on the 15th hole, a 180-yard par-3 into the wind, the caddie handed the golfer a 4 wood, and the golfer balked.

"I think it's a 3 iron," said the golfer.

"No, sir, it's a 4 wood," said the caddie.

"Nope, it's definitely a 3 iron."

So the golfer set up, took the 3 iron back slowly, and struck the ball perfectly. It tore through the wind, hit softly on the front of the green, and rolled up two feet short of the pin.

"See," said the caddie. "I told you it wasn't enough club."

· · · · · · · · · · · · ·

*A*mateur: *How do you get so much backspin?*
Pro: *Before I answer that, tell me, how far do you hit a 5 iron?*
Amateur: *About 130 yards.*
Pro: *Then why in the world would you want the ball to spin back?*

> **"It is nothing new or original to say that golf is played one stroke at a time. But it took me many strokes to realize it."**
>
> **—Former golf legend Robert Trent Jones, Jr.**

mmm. Tough decision. You only have time for one or the
other. Do you want to spend your Saturday afternoon playing
golf or baseball? Now you can do both.

Bat-N Putt is a game developed by Larry Cramton of Marlow,
Oklahoma. It is a combination of the best features of baseball and golf.
Essentially, the equipment is an aluminum baseball bat that has a
squared off chunk at the end and a flat surface used to putt a ball.

He got the idea from an experience he and his buddies had when
teen-agers. "My brother and I grew up around a golf driving range,
baseball pitching machine and a miniature golf course," he said. "We
would invite our friends over to play miniature golf, but they wouldn't
do it. They knew we were so good we would beat them easily. So to
make the games interesting, my brother and I would use a baseball bat
instead of a putter."

The game is played on a regulation golf course (when the pro or
members aren't watching) or any homemade backyard course. Toss a
golf ball, tennis ball or baseball into the air and smack it with the bat.
Or use a portable baseball tee. Go to the point where the ball comes to
rest and hit it again. Once you get to the green, use the flat portion of
the bat to putt the ball into the hole.

Cramton offers a whole line of products, from bats in five sizes to
caps, tees, bags, shirts and soft stitched balls. The "ballclubs" sell for
$59 each.

For more information, call Bat-N Putt at (405) 658-6684.

*S teve was an avid golfer and was trying to determine which golf
course was the best. He narrowed down his selections to
Pinehurst, Augusta National and Pebble Beach. He made arrangements to play each course sot that he could decide which one was the
best.*

*When he got to Pinehurst, he hooked up with three elderly
members. For the entire round they showed him the intricate design
of the course and the natural beauty. Finally, they reached the 18th
tee.*

"What's that?" Steve asked, pointing to a red telephone at the edge of the tee box. "Oh, that's a hotline to God," said one of the members. Steve asked if he could use it.

"Sure, but it'll cost you $100," the member replied. Steve figured he needed some help on the final hole so he pulled out his wallet and paid the 100 bucks. He eagled the final hole.

The following week Steve was at Augusta National. He joined up with three members and had a thoroughly enjoyable round, hearing stories of Bobby Jones and the many Masters tournaments. Finally, they reached the 18th tee.

"What's that?" Steve asked, pointing to a red telephone at the edge of the tee box.

"Oh, that's a hotline to God," said one of the members. Steve asked if he could use it.

"Sure, but it'll cost you $100," the member replied. Steve figured he needed some help on the final hole, so he pulled out his wallet and paid the 100 bucks. He birdied the final hole.

The following week, Steve was at Pebble Beach. He joined up with three members and had a breathtaking experience on the coast of the Pacific Ocean. Finally, they reached the 18th tee.

"What's that?" Steve asked, pointing to a red telephone at the edge of the tee box.

"Oh, that's a hotline to God," said one of the members. Steve asked if he could use it.

"Sure, but it'll cost you 35 cents," the member replied.

"Wait a second," Steve said. "I just paid $100 at Pinehurst and $100 at Augusta National to use the hotline to God. Why does Pebble Beach only charge 35 cents?"

The member looked at Steve and said, "At Pebble Beach, it's a local call."

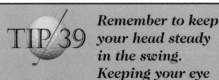

TIP 39 Remember to keep your head steady in the swing. Keeping your eye on the ball is not the same as keeping your head still. If your head moves, concentrate on keeping the back of your neck in place throughout the swing.

HOLE 9

Make your round of golf memorable by chronicling it with a Golf Caption Camera.

The one-use 35 millimeter, 18-exposure cameras come with one of six different captions appearing at the bottom of every photo. The captions include "Wild About Golf!", "Golf . . . Share the Experience," and "Golf . . . It's More Than Just a Game."

Custom captions are available for corporate golf outings or country club events.

The camera is available through Fairway Performance Ltd. on Long Island, New York, for $14.99. Call (800) 441-3028 to find a retail outlet closest to you (or to bulk order).

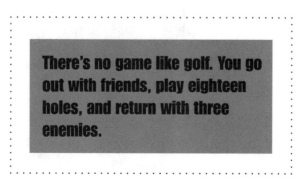

There's no game like golf. You go out with friends, play eighteen holes, and return with three enemies.

*T*he golfer hit his drive into the adjacent water hazard on the first hole.

He walked over to look for his ball and saw it about six feet out from the shore in shallow water.

He took his ball retriever from his bag, extended it and reached out into the water and got his ball. As he was drying it off, he heard a voice speak to him. "Hey, mister," the voice said. He looked around and saw no one.

He started back to drop his ball along the ball's line of flight as it went into the hazard.

"Hey, mister," the voice said again.

He looked down amongst the weeds and grass growing by the water and saw a frog.

This time he was looking at the frog when it said, "Hey, mister."

"Yeah? What do you want, frog?" he asked.

"Mister, I'm really a beautiful princess, but a wicked witch has put a spell on me and turned me into an ugly frog. If you will pick me up and kiss me, I'll turn back into a beautiful princess. Then you can take me home and we'll make wild passionate love for hours," the frog said.

The man reached down, picked the frog up and put it in his windbreaker pocket. He walked a few yards back down the fairway and dropped his ball preparing for his third shot.

"Hey, mister," the frog called, "aren't you going to kiss me?"

The man took a couple of practice swings with his three-wood and then hit the ball onto the par-4 green.

Walking on towards the green, he said, "No, I'm not going to kiss you. At my age, I'd rather have a talking frog."

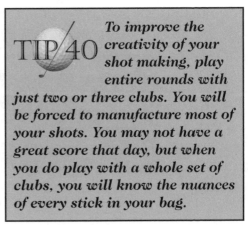

TIP 40

To improve the creativity of your shot making, play entire rounds with just two or three clubs. You will be forced to manufacture most of your shots. You may not have a great score that day, but when you do play with a whole set of clubs, you will know the nuances of every stick in your bag.

*O*ne evening a man and wife were lying in bed.
He was reading and she was watching television and brooding.
"Darling," she started.

"Uh-huh," he replied.

"If I died would you get married again?" she continued.

Knowing this was a trick question, he thought for a moment before answering. "I don't see why not. Our marriage has been a happy one and you'd want me to be happy again, wouldn't you?" he countered laying down his book and taking her hand.

"Yes, I suppose," she answered.

They continued in silence for a while, he with his reading and she watching television and continuing to brood.

"Darling," she started again.

"Uh-huh," he replied.

"If you got married again, would you let your new wife wear my dresses?"

He put his book down and once again took her hand. Again realizing this was a loaded question with no correct answer, he thought for a moment and answered. "I guess I would. After all, it would be a shame just to throw away those nice clothes of yours."

They lapsed back into silence. The reading and more brooding continued.

"Darling," she once again started.

"Yes?" he replied.

"Would you let her wear my shoes?"

This time without putting his book aside, he said, "Yes, and for the same reason. It would be a shame to throw away all your expensive shoes."

Yet again they lapsed back into silence.

"Darling," she said, renewing the inquisition.

"Uh-huh," he replied.

"Would you let her use my new Ping golf clubs?"

With no hesitation, he answered, "Of course not, she's left-handed."

*I*f your favorite course is too crowded to play on weekends, then wait until it gets dark. The golfers will leave and the course is all yours—provided you have a NITELITE golf ball.

The one-piece, cut-proof ball plays like a regulation ball and glows in the dark. A replaceable lightstick lasts for about six hours. However, without the aid of additional lightsticks to show you the fairway, green and hole, you're taking a shot in the dark.

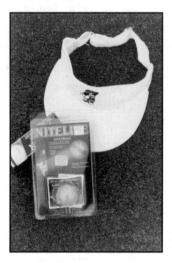

The ball, which sells for about $8, was judged "Most Innovative" at a PGA show and has been featured in *Golf Digest*, *Golf Magazine* and *Sports Illustrated*.

There is an annual national championship and local outings throughout the nation.

NITELITE Golf Balls are produced by C.N. is Believing, based in Wolfeboro Falls, New Hampshire, (800) 282-1533.

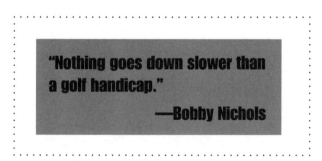

"Nothing goes down slower than a golf handicap."

—Bobby Nichols

I was playing at a nearby course which had caddies. My caddie was about 65 years old and halfway blind. We tee off on the first hole, walk up to my ball and my caddie says, "Oh, Mr. Jones, Mr. Jones, Mr. Jones, that was one of the finest shots I ever done see. Did I mention that I caddied for Mr. Arnold Palmer yesterday, and he hit the very same shot in the very same place as you?"

I ask for my 8 iron, and hit three inches from the pin. When we got there, my caddie says, "Oh, Mr. Jones, Mr. Jones, Mr. Jones, that was one of the finest shots I ever done see. Did I mention that I caddied for Mr. Arnold Palmer yesterday and

TIP 41 Replace your clubs' grips as often as necessary. If you aren't sure whether your grips need replacing, check with a pro. Slick grips force you to hold the club too tightly. That throws off the rest of your swing.

he hit the very same shot in the exact same spot as you?"

I putt out and tee off the second hole, and when we get to my drive, my caddie says, "Oh, Mr. Jones, Mr. Jones, Mr. Jones, that was a fine shot if I ever done see one. Did I mention that I caddied for Mr. Arnold Palmer yesterday and he hit his drive in the same spot as you?"

Then I say, "What club did Arnie hit?"

To this the caddie replied, "Eight iron." So, I take my eight and hit it about thirty yards short and then I ask, "Where did Arnie hit his eight iron?"

The caddie answered, "About thirty yards short."

So there's a guy who golfs with his buddies every weekend, and his wife keeps bugging him to take her along and teach her to play.

He finally relents, and the following Sunday finds them on the first tee. She's never played, so he tells her to go down to the ladies tees, watch him drive, and then try to do like he did.

She goes down to the reds, the guy hooks his drive, and the ball hits his wife, killing her.

The police come to investigate, and the coroner says, "It's the damnedest thing I ever saw. There's an imprint on her temple, and you can read "Titleist 1.""

"That was my ball," the guy said.

"What I don't understand," the coroner continued, "is the one on her hip that says "Titleist 3."

"Oh," the guy replied, "that was my mulligan."

Don't be limited to hitting chip shots in your back yard. Take full swings and hit drivers with the Tru-Shot Air Flow Practice Golf Ball.

Unlike traditional "Whiffle" balls, the Air Flow Practice Golf Ball uses a radical design to give a better feel and truer flight characteristics. The white plastic ball was selected by *Golf Illustrated* as one of the 10 best training aids; *Golf* magazine rated it three-and-a-half stars (out of a possible four).

A package of three balls sells for about $3. It is made by Covington Plastics, Inc. of Cocoa, Florida.

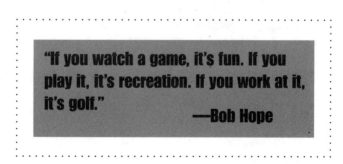

"If you watch a game, it's fun. If you play it, it's recreation. If you work at it, it's golf."

—Bob Hope

*T*wo *young friends learned golf in high school and played a lot together.*

After high school they got jobs and proceeded to bet with each other. They were pretty equally matched so first one would win and then the other would win. As a matter of fact, at the end of the year neither was financially ahead of the other.

As life went on they made more money at their jobs and increased the size of their bets. Still one would win and then the other would win. As usual, at the end of the year, neither was financially ahead of the other.

They became aged and decided to hang up the clubs but would play one last game for $10,000 as each was independently wealthy.

On the 18th tee the match was tied.

One hit a beautiful drive down the middle and the other sliced into the woods.

They looked for the ball for 15 or 20 minutes and the fellow on the fairway said, "I'm going to hit up!"

"OK," said the other, "but I'll keep on looking."

The fellow in the fairway hit one of the best shots of his life and the ball rolled to within six inches of the cup. As he approached the green and got his putter from his caddie, the fellow in the woods shouted, "I found it!"

"Hit it then," said the fellow on the green.

The guy in the woods hacked at the ball. It bounded off a branch, flew the trap, hit on the apron, rolled onto the green and into the cup—at which time the fellow on the green said to his caddie, "What do I do now? I've got his first ball in my pocket!"

If you often lose your balance on the downswing, try opening your left foot from the target line. That makes it easier for you to unwind and maintain your balance throughout the swing.

*I*n an effort to learn the game, two buddies decided to head for the
driving range. There, Eddie would teach Rick how to make the
best use of his clubs.

Rick paid for some oversized buckets of balls and headed for the
tee pad. Repeatedly, he tried to find the sweet spot. After about 20
flails at the ball, he became enraged. He told Eddie and others in the
vicinity to move away; he was about to annihilate the ball.

He assumed a steady stance, drove and followed through perfectly.
As the ball took flight, it connected with a wayward crow which had
maneuvered into "protected air space."

The ball was too much for the bird. Both came crashing back to
terra firma. The bird lost.

Rick was ecstatic. Eddie simply deadpanned, "Congratulations,
my man. We'll score that as your first birdie!"

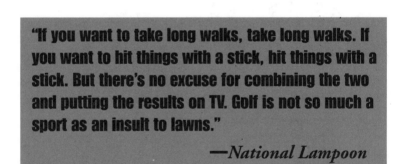

"If you want to take long walks, take long walks. If
you want to hit things with a stick, hit things with a
stick. But there's no excuse for combining the two
and putting the results on TV. Golf is not so much a
sport as an insult to lawns."

—*National Lampoon*

*T*he Golf Mate is a portable indoor, one-ball driving range for
your home or office. It allows you to hit a real golf ball at full
velocity. However, the instructions suggest you don't hit any
club with more loft than a six-iron. Regardless of how hard you hit the
ball, Golf Mate removes the energy from the ball. Then, the ball is

returned to an "organizer" where it is ready for you to use again. Even if you hit a slice or hook, the specially designed angled net will catch every shot.

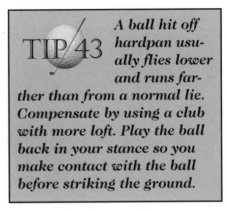

TIP 43

A ball hit off hardpan usually flies lower and runs farther than from a normal lie. Compensate by using a club with more loft. Play the ball back in your stance so you make contact with the ball before striking the ground.

Golf Mate is five-and-a-half feet high, four-and-a-half feet wide, eight feet long and weighs 25 pounds. The frame is made of heavy gauge aluminum square tubing, heavy gauge steel tubing and composite joints. The absorption mat is a highly durable mesh made from polyester threads covered with abrasive resistant PVC. You do not need any tools to assemble the Golf Mate and assembly takes just a few minutes.

Golf Mate is available for $249.95 (plus shipping and handling) through Affordable Golf of Virginia Beach, (757) 425-GOLF..

*T*wo long-time golfers were standing overlooking the river getting ready to hit their shots. One golfer looked to the other and said, *"Look at those idiots fishin' in the rain."*

· · · · · · · · · · · · · · · ·

A couple whose passion had waned saw a marriage counselor and went through a number of appointments that brought little success.

Suddenly at one session the counselor grabbed the wife and kissed her passionately.

"There" he said to the husband, "That's what she needs every Monday, Wednesday, Saturday and Sunday."

"Well," replied the husband, "I can bring her in on Mondays and Wednesdays, but Saturdays and Sundays are my golf days."

HOLE 10

There are many putters on the market today, but few are made with the natural beauty of solid persimmon. Persimmon Pride of Kentucky, Inc. makes a line of such clubs.

The wood of each head is solid persimmon, one of nature's hardest woods. It is specifically cut to maximize its grain and natural hardness. The wood is kiln dried and oil hardened to remove moisture and preserve the wood. The heads are designed to be larger than normal which magnifies the hitting area's sweet spot and helps to produce a low, smooth stroke. The sole of each putter is hand ground and finished from solid brass to its final form.

The putters come in a variety of sizes and styles, ranging from $175 to $250.

For more information, call (513) 272-1913.

Playing solo, George approached the tee and asked the foursome there if it would be OK for him to play through.

Oh, yes. Did we mention George was a deaf-mute?

As was his practice, the question was written on paper. Handing it over, the foursome passed it to one another. The fourth of the group laughed heartily and tore George's request into confetti. The others were convulsed by hysteria.

At the ninth hole, George was rankled by the plodding play of the group. Exasperated, he launched a shot down the fairway just as one from the foursome attempted his second shot. It buzzed the scalp of the guy who ripped up George's request.

> **TIP/44**
>
> **If you have trouble getting the ball up in the air, try moving the ball forward in your stance, open the club face slightly and release your wrists as you make contact with the ball.**

Turning around, the foursome looked back to the tee.

There stood George, all smiles, with four fingers held aloft!

. . . .

*A*ll his life, a most proper and dignified English barrister widower, with a considerable income, had dreamed of playing Sandringham, one of Great Britain's truly exclusive golf courses.

One day he made up his mind to chance it while he was traveling in the area.

Although he was aware that the club was very exclusive, he decided that he would ask the man behind the desk if he might play the famous course. The club's secretary inquired, "Member ?"

"No, sir."

"Guest of a member?"

"No, sir."

"Sorry," the secretary said.

As he turned to leave, the lawyer spotted a slightly familiar figure seated in the lounge reading the London Times. *It was Lord Willoughby Parham.*

The lawyer approached Lord Parham and, bowing low, said, "I beg your pardon, your Lordship, but my name is Higginbotham of the London Solicitor, Higginbotham and Barclay. I should like to ask your Lordship's indulgence. Might I play this beautiful course as your guest?"

His Lordship gave Higginbotham a long look, put down his paper and his pipe and asked: "Church?"

"Church of England, sir, as was my late wife."

"Education?" the elderly gentleman asked.

"Eton, sir, and Oxford with a Blue and Honors."

"Sport?" "Rugby, sir, spot of tennis and number four on the crew that beat Cambridge."

"Service?" "Brigadier, sir, Coldstream Guards, Victoria Cross and Knights of the Garter."

"Campaigns?" "Dunkirk, El Alemain and Normandy, sir."

"Languages?"

"Private tutor in French, fluent in German and a bit of Greek."

His Lordship considered briefly, then nodded to the club secretary and said, "Nine Holes."

U se the latest radar technology to test the speed of your swing. A consistent swing speed means consistent shot making. The SwingMate will help identify your most powerful and consistent swing and let you duplicate that swing. Simply place the SwingMate three or four feet behind the tee and in line with the direction of the stroke. Swing and a digital display indicates the club head speed (in miles per hour), as well as the distance the ball should travel (if stroked properly).

The SwingMate sells for $95. It is available through Gadgets & Gizmos of Lawrenceville, Georgia, (800) 553-1841.

T he worst (and wealthiest) member of Augusta National approached Ben Crenshaw after The Masters.

Challenging Gentle Ben to a match, the member set the stakes at double or nothing the dough that Crenshaw had just pocketed.

Crenshaw debated silently. Twice the money? It was a no-brainer. And to level the playing field, so to speak, Crenshaw told the member he could claim any handicap he wished.

The member requested 2 Gottchas. Crenshaw wasn't sure what a gottcha was, but since the man was insistent he complied.

They went to the first tee, where the member uncorked a

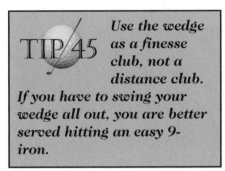

TIP/45 Use the wedge as a finesse club, not a distance club. **If you have to swing your wedge all out, you are better served hitting an easy 9-iron.**

slice of incomprehensible proportion. Crenshaw teed his ball. The member slithered up behind Gentle Ben, swung his drive hard between Crenshaw's legs and bellowed, "Gottcha!"

At the end of the round, those on hand were stunned to learn Crenshaw had lost the match.

In self-defense, he asked the onlookers: "Which of you ever played a round waiting for the second 'gottcha?'"

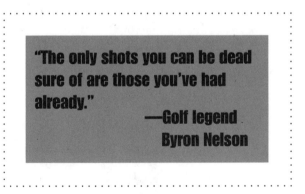

"The only shots you can be dead sure of are those you've had already."

—Golf legend
Byron Nelson

f the grips on your clubs feel small and you don't want to have all of them re-gripped, then consider using Add-On.

It's a pliable, self-adhesive, single-sheet material that provides any golfer with an easy, accurate and fast way of building up a grip on any club. The only tools you will need are your hands and a utility knife.

Add-On comes in a variety of thicknesses, from 1/32nd of an inch to 1/64th of an inch. It sells for $5.50 to $9.50 per pack.

Add-On is based in Elyria, Ohio, and can be reached by calling (440) 366-0918.

A terrible golfer was playing a round for which he had hired a caddie.

The round proved to be somewhat tortuous for the caddie to watch, and he was getting a bit exasperated by the poor play of his employer.

At one point, the ball lay about 180 yards from the green, as the golfer sized up his situation he asked his caddie, "Do you think I can get there with a 5-iron?"

The caddie replied, "Eventually."

· · · · · · · · · · · ·

J im is such a good golfer. . .

He really has improved. Today he hit the ball in one!

He screamed "fore" when he putted!

He just missed a hole-in-one by a measly seven strokes.

He was sent to the shrink because he believes the sport actually is a game.

He always cheats. When he scores a hole-in-one, it gets marked with a zero on his card.

T here's a young caddie named Junior who hangs out at the local golf course. The caddie master doesn't know what Junior's problem is, but the other caddies like to tease him. They say he is two bricks short of a

TIP 46

If you have difficulty taking your putter straight back, it might be caused by tension in your hands or forearms. If so, try a forward press. Move your wrists forward an inch or two, then take your hands back in a straight line.

load, or two pickles shy of a barrel. To prove it, sometimes the caddies offer Junior his choice between a nickel and a dime. He always takes the nickel, they say, because it's bigger.

One day after Junior grabbed the nickel, the caddie master got him off to one side and said, "Junior, those caddies are making fun of you. They think you don't know the dime is worth more than the nickel. Are you grabbing the nickel because it's bigger, or what?"

Junior said, "Well, if I took the dime, they'd quit doing it!"

> "Relax? How can anybody relax and play golf? You have to grip the club don't you?"
>
> —Ben Hogan

Green Grass Golf Corp. of Hicksville, New York, offers new technology in a number of club designs.

It used the architectural attributes of bridges to design its unique putter. Green Grass claims, "We all know the fact that the arch bridge design can distribute the load on the bridge evenly throughout the whole bridge area. The loaded weight (or force) is transferred to the two ends of the bridge support evenly. We are the first to incorporate this concept onto a golf club."

Green Grass makes pendulum balanced putters called Sigma and Theta. The company claims that when the center of gravity on any putter head "is lined up with the golf ball at impact, the maximum amount of energy is released. It would be unheard of to actually be able to change the center of gravity on a putter! But we have done the unthinkable. The center of gravity . . . can be changed by maneuvering the weight plates, thus drastically shifting the center of gravity toward the toe or toward the heel of the putter. You can change the center of gravity to match your own style of putt by redistributing the weight on the putter head without adding extra weight."

The Sigma has a steel black head and weighs 500 grams. The Theta has a brass head and weighs slightly less. Both sell for $70 each.

Green Grass also makes the Sneaky Long II driver. According to the club's manual, the driver "is the first and only club in the world utilizing a non-welded/locking design, which

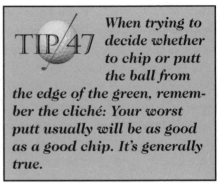

When trying to decide whether to chip or putt the ball from the edge of the green, remember the cliché: Your worst putt usually will be as good as a good chip. It's generally true.

consists of an internal reinforcing element (optional) and a deflectable face plate. A unique, mechanically compressed joint is established where the insert face meets the club head. This allows the two materials to be locked together without welding."

The driver also incorporates an air foil design at the toe and crown that effectively reduces the ground effect and down wash. It sells for $120.

For more information, call Green Grass at (516) 935-6722, extension 10.

A *grandfather and grandson were playing golf together. On a severely dog-legged par-4, the grandfather told the grandson, "When I was your age, I'd aim right over those trees and hit the green every time."*

The grandson thought about that comment and decided to give it a try. He hit a perfect drive, but it landed right in the middle of the 50-foot trees.

The grandson looked sadly at the grandfather who said, "Of course when I was your age, those trees were eight feet tall."

· · · · · · · · · · · · ·

B *rian had tried to be particularly careful about his language as he played golf with his preacher.*

But on the 12th hole, when he twice failed to hit out of a sand trap, he lost his resolve and let fly with a string of expletives.

The preacher felt obliged to respond. "I have observed," said he in a calm voice, "that the best golfers do not use foul language."

"I guess not," said Brian. "What the hell do they have to cuss about?"

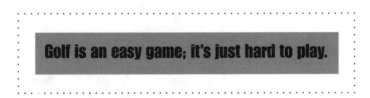

Golf is an easy game; it's just hard to play.

A fellow goes to the doctor and says, "Doc, every time I swing my 7 iron I pass outrageous gas."

He swings the iron in the doctor's office and breaks a loud pass of wind.

He swings the 8 iron and nothing, he swings the 6 and nothing. He swings the 7; again the same loud sound is heard, followed by a very foul smell.

The doctor says, "Hmm, interesting case," and gets up and grabs a long pole laying against the wall.

"What are you going to do with that?" the fellow nervously asks, fearing the worst.

"I'm going to open the window and let some air into this room," the doctor replies.

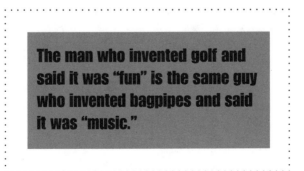

The man who invented golf and said it was "fun" is the same guy who invented bagpipes and said it was "music."

Avoid banging your club heads together in your golf bag by using the Deluxe Club Rack with Putter Holder.

The rugged plastic holder organizes your clubs and protects the heads at the same time. It is designed to keep your clubs from falling out of the bag, too. You can attach the rack in minutes on virtually any sized bag.

There is room for seven irons on the main rack, plus attachments for two wedges and a putter. It sells for about $30.

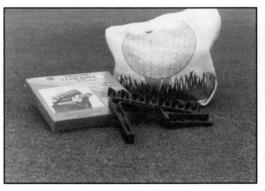

The Deluxe Club Rack is manufactured by Double Products Co. based in Manhattan Beach, California, (310) 546-1154.

*L*ady Luck was seldom kind to Bob.
Although Bob had a real zest for life he was constantly beset by bad luck.

He loved poker but poker did not love Bob; he played the stock market with great anticipation but always seemed to be the one who bought high and sold low. His life seemed to be full of more downs than ups.

Ah, but his greatest delight was his golf game. Not that Bob was a great golfer; in fact, he never managed to break 100, but the odd shot that somehow ended up in the general area he had in mind was enough to keep his hopes alive.

Finally Bob became ill and passed away. But just before he died, he asked that his remains be cremated and his ashes be scattered just off the fairway on the ninth hole of his home course.

Accordingly, a gathering assembled to carry out Bob's wishes. It was a bright sunny day and was going well.

Then, as the ashes were being strewn, a gust of wind came up and blew Bob out of bounds.

. . . .

*J*oe *had a particularly bad day on the course. Nothing went right and he became more angry with each passing hole.*

By the par-3 17th hole, he was fit to be tied and when he missed a two-foot putt (for a double bogey), he really exploded.

Letting loose a stream of expletives the likes of which had never been heard before or since, Joe proceeded to toss his clubs into the lake and set his golf cart on fire.

Declaring that he would never play this game again, Joe stomped off to the clubhouse, into the locker room and proceeded to cut his wrists.

At that point one of the club members happened in and, not noticing Joe's desperate condition, off-handedly said , "Hey, Joe, we need a fourth for tomorrow morning. How 'bout it?"

Joe looked up and said, "What time?"

TIP 48 **Do not assume that you are centering the ball on the club face at address. Have someone check the placement for you every now and then on the range. If you aren't centered, it will be difficult to get consistency in your game.**

HOLE 11

 ositive Putter Co., Inc. of Indianapolis, has created a line of clubs that it claims as the "World's Best Balanced Putters." Their tests show that Positive Putters enable the club face to remain square to the target line while stationary or in motion. One of the models also includes alternate striking dots for fast or slow greens. One dot shows the sweet spot. Strike the ball at another dot and it reduces the energy for a slower roll and more control.

The putters list for $199 each. To order a Positive Putter, call (800) 274-2322.

A golfer, having been taken by a hustler at the club which left him $1,000 poorer, was driving down the highway when he saw a priest at the side of the road. He stopped to pick up the priest and give him a ride. As the priest climbed in, they instantly recognized one another. The priest had played in the foursome behind the man.

A ways down the road the golfer saw the player who had swindled him out of the $1,000. He directed his sport utility vehicle right at the swindler. Then he thought better of it, given the companion riding to his right. At the last second, the golfer maneuvered his SUV to miss the swindler. Still, he heard a loud thump. He had a

TIP/49 Use the upper body's muscles to take the club back in your swing. But use the lower body's muscles to bring the club forward in your swing.

sick feeling in his stomach. He looked in his rear-view mirror, but didn't see anything.

He turned to the priest and said, "Sorry, Father, I just missed that swindler at the side of the road."

Said the priest, "Don't worry son, I got him with my door."

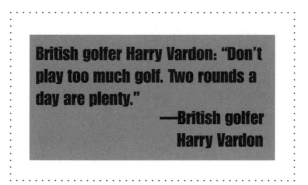

British golfer Harry Vardon: "Don't play too much golf. Two rounds a day are plenty."

—British golfer Harry Vardon

*O*n the train to a sporting goods convention, a group of golfers and a group of tennis players sat in the same car. Each of the tennis players had his/her train ticket, but it became clear that the group of golfers had only one ticket amongst them. The tennis players started laughing and snickering.

When one of the golfers said, "Here comes the conductor," all of the golfers went into the bathroom. The tennis players were puzzled.

The conductor came aboard, said, "tickets please," and collected tickets from all the tennis players. He then went to the bathroom, knocked on the door and said, "ticket please," and the golfers stuck the ticket under the door. The conductor took it and left, and the golfers came out of the bathroom a few minutes later. The tennis players felt really stupid.

So, on the way back from the convention, the group of tennis players had one ticket for the group. They started snickering at the golfers, for this time the whole group had no tickets amongst them. When the golfer lookout said, "Conductor coming!", all the golfers went into the bathroom. All the tennis players went into another bathroom, knocked on the other bathroom, and said, "ticket, please."

. . . .

A man and his wife were playing golf with another couple at their club.

They came to a par-4, dog-leg left. The man pulled his drive to the left and hit it behind a storage barn.

His friend said, "If you open the front door and the back door of the barn, you'll have a clear shot to the green."

So they opened the doors and the man took his shot. It rattled through the rafters of the barn, shot out through a window, hit his wife on the head and killed her!

It was 10 years before the man could get the courage to play the course again.

Sure enough, he got to the same hole, pulled his drive again and ended up behind the same storage barn.

The man he was playing with this time said, "If you open the front door and the back door of the barn, you'll have a clear shot to the green."

The man said, "I don't think so. The last time I tried that, something terrible happened."

"What was that?" asked his friend.

The man replied, "I got a seven!"

If you would rather watch golf than play it, then consider buying a portable seat. Whether you are following your favorite group or staying at one hole to watch every golfer, you will be much more comfortable with a seat.

The one-legged Spectator Seat Stick is the most portable, most widely used seat at golf tournaments throughout the nation. A collapsible reinforced leather seat sits atop a chromium steel pointed shaft that digs firmly into the ground. It takes only a moment to put it in place and only another moment to fold it up and carry it to the next location.

The adjustable rod allows comfortable use by fans of all heights. The seat sells at most golf shops for about $24.

"My best score ever was 103, but I've only been playing 15 years."

—Ex-NFL star Alex Karras

---

*T*he clubhouse bar was so sure that its bartender was the strongest man around, that it offered a stading $5,000 bet. The bartender woud squeeze a lemon until all the juice ran into a glass, and hand the lemon to a golfer. Anyone who could squeeze one more drop *of juice out would win the money. Many golfers had tried over time but nobody could do it.*

One day a despicable little man, dressed in loud golf attire, came in saying, "I'd like to try the bet."

After the laughter died down, the bartender said OK, grabbed a lemon and squeezed away. Then he handed the wrinkled remains of the rind to the little man. The crowd's laughter turned to total silence as the man clenched his fist around the lemon and six drops fell into the glass.

As the crowd cheered, the bartender paid the $5,000, and asked the little man, "What do you do for a living? Are you a lumberjack, a weight lifter, or what?"

The man replied, "When I'm not playing golf, I work for the IRS."

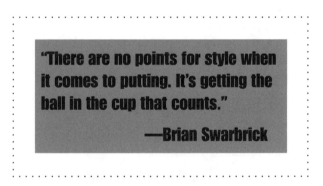

"There are no points for style when it comes to putting. It's getting the ball in the cup that counts."

—Brian Swarbrick

A buddy was playing in a tournament in Arizona last fall. His caddie had been cackling and snickering after every shot. Upset over the blatant disrespect, he finally threw his putter at the caddie and exclaimed, "You must be the worst caddie in the world."

The caddie grinned, "That, my good man, would be too great of a coincidence."

The Iron Hooker allows a golfer to organize clubs in virtually any sized bag. Aligned along the outside of the bag, irons rest in place, leaving plenty of room in the center for your woods and putter. Weighing just six ounces, the Iron Hooker attaches in minutes and has an add-on lock to keep clubs from falling out when you travel.

The Iron Hooker is available for $29.95 from Iron Hooker Inc. of LaPorte, Indiana, (800) 731-2961.

TIP 50

To feel proper balance at the start of a swing, pretend you are a shortstop. To be able to move in any direction quickly, you wouldn't have your feet too far apart or too close together. You wouldn't have your weight too far forward or backward. Be balanced on the balls of your feet with a natural flex in your knees.

Hey, Joe Golfer: The results are in, and after 20 years of playing golf, it boils down to this:

Approximate number of holes: 30,000

Holes-in-one: 0

Eagles: 0

Birdies: 1,000

Pars: 3,000

Bogeys or worse: 20,000 or more

Putters used: 30

Drivers used: 100

Iron sets used: 50

Lessons with conflicting instruction: 100

Gave up before completing round: 50

Hit by ball without hearing "fore": 5

Average good shots per round: 4

Average lousy shots per round: 90
Lowest handicap: 18
Lowest score: 83 (no, NOT on the front nine)
Highest score: 126
Shanks per round: 1, usually more
Topped or fat shots per round: 25
Back sprains or muscle pulls: 12
Times game was "quit" for more than a month: 5
Balls purchased: 2,000
Balls lost: 1,000
Wives lost: 4
Children you don't know: 6

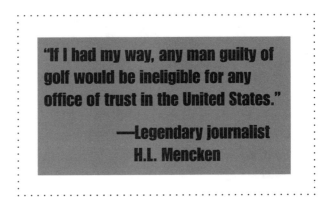

"If I had my way, any man guilty of golf would be ineligible for any office of trust in the United States."

—Legendary journalist H.L. Mencken

*B*ubba was hired as the new assistant pro at a small municipal course in North Dakota. Bubba says to the head pro, "Boss, I know everyone that ever mattered in the world of golf!

The head pro doesn't believe him, so he says, "No, you do not know everyone that ever mattered in the world of golf."

But Bubba says, "Yes I do!"

So the head pro says, "Well, prove it!"

Bubba says, "Pick someone, and I know them!"

Well, the head pro thinks for a minute and then comes up with a name. "Tiger Woods!" I bet you don't know Tiger Woods!"

Bubba says, "Tiger Woods! Tiger and I played with each other in the Junior World Tournament!"

The head pro says, "No, you didn't"!"

Bubba says, "Yes, I did."

So they fly to Orlando and drive up to Tiger Woods' house. Bubba knocks on the door and Tiger answers and Bubba goes "Tiger!" and Tiger goes "Bubba!" and they hug and catch up for 30 minutes and the head pro can't believe it.

But then he thinks, that could happen, it's just one person, so he tells Bubba and Bubba says, "OK, pick somebody else!"

This time the head pro has someone in mind.

"Ben Crenshaw! You do not know Ben Crenshaw!"

But Bubba says, "Oh yes I do! Ben and I teamed together to beat a pair of Scotsmen in a tournament a couple of years ago."

The head pro says, "No, you didn't!"

Bubba says, "Yes, I did!"

So they fly to Texas and they catch Ben Crenshaw at the driving range prior to a tournament. They work their way through the crowd until Bubba gets close enough to catch Crenshaw's eye and waves, "Ben! " and Crenshaw waves, "Bubba!"

After Crenshaw finished hitting balls, he came over to Bubba and the two hug and catch up for 30 minutes and the head pro is stunned. He can't believe it.

But then he thinks—that's just two people, it doesn't mean he knows everyone that matters in the world of golf. So he tells Bubba and Bubba says, "OK, pick someone out of the world spectrum and I know them!"

And the head pro knows just who to pick so he says, "Jack Nicklaus! You do not know Jack Nicklaus!"

Bubba says, "Jack Nicklaus! I gave lessons to Jack Nicklaus just last summer !"

TIP 51 Remember to compensate for the draw on a shot taken from a side hill lie with your feet lower than the ball. If your feet are higher than the ball, compensate for a fade.

The head pro says, "No, you didn't!"

Bubba says, "Yes, I did!"

So they fly to Columbus where Nicklaus is just about to tee off in a big tournament. They work their way through the crowd, without much luck, so Bubba says, "Boss, we're never gonna get there together through all these people, so I tell you what, I'll work my way up there and when I do, I'll give you a sign that shows you I know Jack!" and he leaves.

The head pro waits and waits and waits, and just when he's about to give up, he sees Jack Nicklaus walking up the first fairway and right there beside him is Bubba! Shortly afterwards, the head pro passes ut.

Bubba comes back and finds the head pro on ground, so he fans him and says, "Wake up!" and when the head pro comes to, he asks, "What happened?!!"

The head pro looks at Bubba and says, "OK, I can see Tiger Woods. I can see Ben Crenshaw. Hell, I can even see Jack Nicklaus! But when somebody standing next to me asks, 'Who's that up there with Bubba?' That's a little more than I can take!"

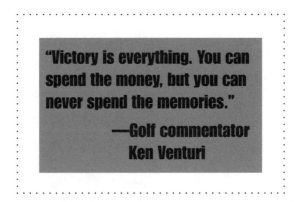

"Victory is everything. You can spend the money, but you can never spend the memories."

—Golf commentator Ken Venturi

Don't buy a golf bag and a pull cart. Get Golf Mate, a bag and cart combined.

The Golf Mate weighs just 15 pounds and has an aluminum frame and nylon pockets. Your clubs fit easily into a wide compartment and there are spots for an umbrella, balls, gloves and rain gear. There's even a fold down seat. With clubs, it fits easily into a car trunk. Without clubs, it folds for easy storage. It sells for $149.95.

Golf Mate Carts is based in Rye, New York, (800) 868-4194.

*T*wo friends were playing golf one day. They decided that they would adhere strictly to the rules, i.e., no improving the lie.

After a few holes, one guy's ball landed on a cart path. As he reached down to pick up his ball to get relief his friend said, "We agreed that we would not improve our lie."

No matter how much the first fellow tried to explain that he was entitled to this relief, the second fellow would not allow it.

So the man went to the cart to get a club. As he stood over the ball he took a few practice swings, each time scraping the club on the pavement, taking out big chunks of blacktop and sending out lots of sparks! Finally, after several practice swings he took his shot.

The ball took off and landed on the green about six feet from the pin.

"Great shot!" his friend exclaimed. "What club did you use?"

The man answered, "I used your 7 iron!"

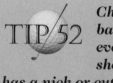

TIP 52 — **Check your ball before every tee shot. If it has a nick or cut, replace it. If it is dirty, clean it. An imperfect ball will not rotate evenly, forcing it to move off center. Save your old balls for backyard practice.**

HOLE 12

I f you want to walk the course, but can't carry your clubs, you are forced to use a caddie or pull cart. If there are no caddies and a pull cart is too heavy for you, what can you do?

Get AutoCaddy, a battery operated, remote-controlled cart that holds any sized golf bag. The cart is equipped with six wheels, an adjustable handle, cruise control, distance timer and a scorecard holder.

It is manufactured by Golf Technologies, Inc. of Natick, Massachusetts, and sells for $520 to $685 (depending on options purchased). For more information, call (800) 200-0373.

After 45 years in the military, most of it in charge of an artillery division, the general finally retired.

He moped around the house for days until his wife, tired of hearing his complaints, told him to get a hobby.

He chose golf. Never having golfed before, he called his former aide who happened to be an avid golfer.

As they stepped up to the tee on the first hole, a beautiful par-4 of 425 yards with a slight dog-leg right, the aide explained to the general that he had to hit the ball to the flag.

The general lined up his shot, took a powerful swing and knocked the ball to just two inches from the cup. The aide was amazed.

As they left the teeing ground and moved toward the green, the aide remarked how great the shot was, it "almost" went in the hole.

TIP/53 Watch the best players in the world and they seldom hit the ball straight. They always are trying to move the ball—under control—one direction or another. Practice hitting fades and draws. To continue improving your score, you must learn to hit every shot called for in a round.

"Almost?" said the general. "What do you mean?"

"Well," explained the aide, "the object is to get the ball into the hole in as few strokes as possible."

Staring at the aide in disgust, the general screamed, "Why the hell didn't you tell me that before?"

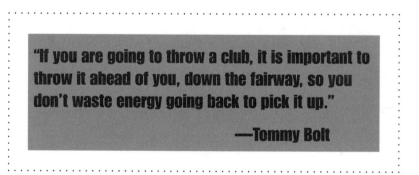

"If you are going to throw a club, it is important to throw it ahead of you, down the fairway, so you don't waste energy going back to pick it up."

—Tommy Bolt

Rained out of your golf game? Then play The Golf Edition of the Monopoly Game. It is the authorized version of the traditional Monopoly Game by Parker Brothers. Instead of landing on Park Place or Illinois Avenue, you'll come to rest on Pinehurst or Torrey Pines.

The object still is the same: Buy tournaments, golf courses and properties of all types; increase the value of your courses and other properties by adding houses and hotels; amass the greatest fortune in money and property, and you are the winner.

As the box says, "With The Golf Edition of the Monopoly Game you can forget about your handicap and stop worrying about determining your slope. You can play in any weather and not be concerned about the length of your shorts or if the course has gone spikeless. You won't find it necessary to play a draw, hit a power fade, choose the right club or blame your caddie when you come up short.

"If you're looking for a break, you might get one with a roll of the dice but not on the green. And, you don't have to worry if there is water on the left, or on the right if you're a southpaw, because the only hook in this game is in getting 'hooked,' on The Golf Edition of the Monopoly Game—a new version of a much revered American institution."

Available for about $30, The Golf Edition is distributed by U.S.A.OPOLY, Inc. and is available in most golf or game stores.

*T*he Pope met with the College of Cardinals to discuss a proposal from Shimon Peres, the former leader of Israel.

"Your holiness," said one of the cardinals, "Mr. Peres wants to determine whether Jews or Catholics are superior, by challenging you to a golf match."

The Pope was greatly disturbed, as he had never held a golf club in his life.

"Not to worry," said the cardinal, "we'll call America and talk to Jack Nicklaus. We'll make him a cardinal; he can play Shimon Peres. We can't lose!"

Everyone agreed it was a good idea. The call was made and, of course, Jack was honored and agreed to play.

The day after the match, Nicklaus reported to the Vatican to inform the Pope of his success in the match.

"I came in second, your Holiness," said Nicklaus.

"Second?" exclaimed the surprised Pope. "You came in second to Shimon Peres?"

"No," said Nicklaus, "second to Rabbi Woods."

· · · · · · · · · · · · · ·

Q: What are the four worst words you could hear during a game of golf?

A: It's still your turn!

· · · · · · · · · · · · · ·

"Doctor, we've got an emergency! My baby just swallowed my golf tees."

"I'll be there at once."

"But tell 'em what to do 'til you get here, Doc."

"Practice your putting."

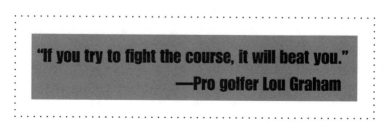

"If you try to fight the course, it will beat you."
—Pro golfer Lou Graham

TIP 54

The only way to know your strengths and weaknesses on a course is to chart your performance. Don't rely on your memory. Golfers have a tendency to remember their great shots, but not the errant ones.
Record more than your hole score on the card. Record whether or not your tee shot landed in the fairway. Record which iron you used on your approach shot and whether or not you hit the green. Then record your number of putts. Analyze your results and devote practice time to areas of your game that need the most help.

---

*A*t a golf course, the four men approached the 16th tee. *The straight fairway ran along a road and bike path fenced off on the left. The first golfer teed off and hooked the ball in that direction.*

The ball went over the fence and bounced off the bike path onto the road, where it hit the tire of a moving bus and was knocked back on to the fairway.

As they all stood in amazement, one man asked him, "How on earth did you do that?"

Without hesitation, he said, "You have to know the bus schedule."

A ristocrat Golf Clubs produce unique, personalized tartan putters which are hand crafted in St. Andrews, Scotland. The clubs are finished with hickory shafts, leather grips and brass sole plates. The putter heads are hand painted to authentically reproduce the design and colors of any tartan selected by the customer. Each putter is complemented with a matching head cover. The putter is priced at $120.

The company also makes a line of shoe bags and head covers in any tartan. Both may be embroidered with your name or monogram. The shoe bag is $25; a set of three head covers is $45.

To contact Aristocrat Golf Clubs in St. Andrews, Scotland, call 44-(0)1334-474217.

*T*wo *women were paired in the tournament and met on the putting green for the first time.*

After introductions, the first golfer asked, "What's your handicap?"

"Oh, I'm a scratch golfer," the other replied.

"Really!" exclaimed the first woman, suitably impressed that she was paired with her.

"Yes, I write down all my good scores and scratch out the bad ones!"

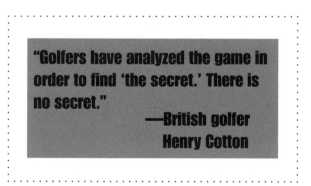

"Golfers have analyzed the game in order to find 'the secret.' There is no secret."

—British golfer
Henry Cotton

A *foursome of senior golfers hit the course with waning enthusiasm for the sport. "These hills are getting steeper as the years go by,"* one complained.

"These fairways seem to be getting longer too," said one of the others.

"The sand traps seem to be bigger than I remember too," said the third senior.

After hearing enough from his Senior buddies, the oldest, and the wisest of the four of them at 87 years old, piped up and said, "Just be thankful we're still on the right side of the grass!"

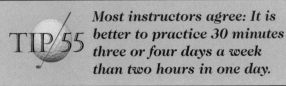

TIP/55 *Most instructors agree: It is better to practice 30 minutes three or four days a week than two hours in one day.*

The ultimate luxury for a golfer might be to have your own miniature golf course in a basement, garage or patio area. With or without the windmill, to create your own miniature golf holes contact Wittek Golf Supply Co., Inc. in Chicago at (800) 869-1800.

Among the supplies you can get are Safe-T-Putters. Available in five different sizes and eight different colors, each putter has machined steel inserts that create the weight and feel of metal putters. The center shaft design can be used for both right and left handed players.

Wittek offers a wide selection of balls that come in bright neon and brilliant pastel colors. It also has unsinkable "floater balls."

If you need carpet for your greens, Wittek has a wide range of grades for heavy and light traffic areas.

And finally, don't forget your personalized pencils, score cards, tee off pads and green cups.

"Golf is a game whose aim is to hit a very small ball into an even smaller hole, with weapons singularly ill-designed for the purpose."

—Former British prime minister Winston Churchill

A man wants to play golf, but shows up at the golf course by himself.

The starter groups him with three ladies, currently on the first hole. Upon walking up to the tee, the man sees the three ladies are nuns. He thinks to himself, "I gotta watch my p's and q's!"

Everyone introduces everyone else on the first tee and one

TIP 56

If you have gone through 29 putters, 47 lessons and dozens of videos, but still can't make a putt, start over. If you are right-handed, become a left-hander. You probably won't start with any bad habits or negative thoughts. Give it a try.

of the nuns says to the man, "Go ahead, sir! You're up."

The man takes a deep breath and proceeds to tee off.

The ball goes down the fairway, hits a rock, and bounces directly to the right into the sand bunker.

The man says, "Jesus Christ! Did you see that?!" forgetting his audience. He is instantly embarrassed when he comes to his senses and one of the nuns says, "We don't talk that way in the presence of the Lord. Watch your language, sir. Now step aside, it's my turn."

The nun winds up and swings as absolutely hard as she can.

The ball slices almost instantly, hits a tree dead center, and bounces out of bounds across the parking lot. The nun bends over, gets her tee, and mutters "God damnit!" as she walks by the man.

The man, rather amused and astonished, says, "Why sister, you just said . . ."

The nun interrupts and finishes, "Yeah, I know what I just said. But then again you didn't just hit a goddamn tree, did you?"

Golf: A five-mile walk punctuated with disappointments.

*T*here were these two guys looking for an errant shot in the woods when they came upon an old, abandoned mine shaft. Curious about its depth, they threw in a tiny pebble and waited for the sound of it striking the bottom, but they heard nothing. They went and got a bigger rock, threw it and waited. Still nothing. They searched the area for something larger and came upon a railroad tie. With great difficulty, the two men carried it to the opening and threw it in. While waiting for it to hit bottom, a goat suddenly darted between them and leapt into the hole!

The guys were still standing there with astonished looks upon their faces from the actions of the goat when a man walked up to them. He asked them if they had seen a goat anywhere in the area and they said that one just jumped into the mine shaft in front of them! The man replied, "Oh no. That couldn't be 'my' goat. Mine was tied to a railroad tie."

· · · · · · · · · · · ·

"You think so much of your old golf game that you don't even remember when we were married," said the pouting wife.

"Of course I do, my dear. It was the day I sank that 30-foot putt."

*I*f you desire a more realistic putting or chipping green for your back yard, then contact Michael Fiore Synthetic Golf Systems, with offices in New Jersey, Chicago and Los Angeles. You can have a professional putting green designed and installed in your back yard. The greens are custom designed to match your back yard.

The surface of the green is a combination of man-made and natural elements that creates the look and play of bent grass greens. On the surface, the ball behaves just as it would on any grass green. You can set the ball speed, holding capabilities and shape to match your favorite course. You even can add chipping pads or sand traps.

Prices vary depending on the location, size and add-ons, but most greens can be built for just $10-$15 per square foot.

For more information, call (847) 432-8130.

A golfer had made an awful shot and tore up a large piece of turf. He picked it up and looking about said, "What shall I do with this?"

"If I were you," said the caddie, "I'd take it home to practice on."

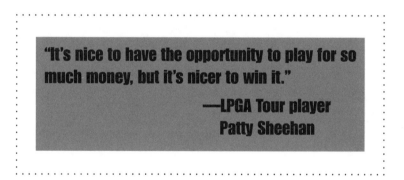

"It's nice to have the opportunity to play for so much money, but it's nicer to win it."

—LPGA Tour player
Patty Sheehan

A woman walked into the bedroom and found her husband in bed with his golf clubs.

Seeing the astonished look on her face, he calmly said, "Well, you said I had to choose, right?"

If you think it's hard to meet new people, pick up the wrong golf ball on the course sometime.

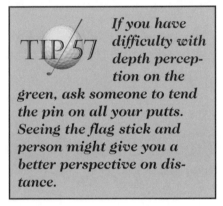

TIP 57 *If you have difficulty with depth perception on the green, ask someone to tend the pin on all your putts. Seeing the flag stick and person might give you a better perspective on distance.*

HOLE 13

O K, so maybe you don't want your own artificial putting green. However, you want your yard to look as pretty as an Augusta fairway or Pebble Beach green. Then you need some professional lawn equipment.

Get your mower, blower and roller from Lawn and Golf. Even if you can't get your lawn to look like a golf course, you can look like a greens keeper with this professional gear.

For about $14,000 you can get a Jacobsen Turfcat Out-Front Rotary Mower.

For about $5,900 you can get a Buffalo Turbine Debris Blower.

And for about $100 you can get a Douglas Products Greensmower Roller.

For more information, call Lawn and Golf of Phoenixville, Pennsylvania, at (610) 933-5801.

Did we mention the sod cutters?

T hree out of town caddies are at the exclusive club's caddie shack, trying to convince the caddie master to hire them. The caddie master says to the first caddie, "What is three times three?"

"274," was his reply.

The caddie master says to the seceond caddie, "It's your turn. What is three times three?"

"Tuesday," replies the second caddie.

The caddie master says to the third caddie, "Okay, your turn. What's three times three?"

"Nine," says the third caddie.

"That's great!" says the caddie master.

"How'd you get that?"

"Simple," says the third caddie. "I subtracted 274 from Tuesday."

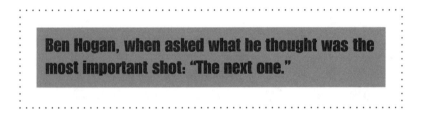

Ben Hogan, when asked what he thought was the most important shot: "The next one."

*S*tevie Wonder and Jack Nicklaus are in a bar. Nicklaus turns to Wonder and says: "How is the singing career going?"

Stevie Wonder says: "Not too bad, the latest album has gone into the top 10 so all in all I think it is pretty good. By the way how's the golf?"

Nicklaus replies: "Not too bad. I'm not winning as much as I used to, but I'm still making a bit of money. I have had some problems with my swing, though."

Stevie Wonder says: "I always find that when my swing goes wrong I need to stop playing for a while

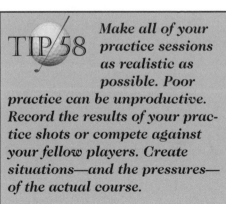

TIP 58 Make all of your practice sessions as realistic as possible. Poor practice can be unproductive. Record the results of your practice shots or compete against your fellow players. Create situations—and the pressures—of the actual course.

and not think about it, then the next time I play it seems to be all right."

Jack Nicklaus says: "You play golf?"

Stevie Wonder says: "Yes, I have been playing for years."

And Nicklaus says: "But I thought you were blind. How can you play golf if you are blind?"

He replies: "I get my caddie to stand in the middle of the fairway and he calls to me. I listen for the sound of his voice and play the ball towards him, then when I get to where the ball lands the caddie moves to the green or further down the fairway. Again I play the ball towards his voice."

"But how do you putt?" says Nicklaus.

"Well," says Stevie, "I get my caddie to lean down in front of the hole and call to me with his head on the ground, and I just play the ball towards his voice."

Nicklaus says: "What is your handicap."

Stevie says, "Well, I play to scratch."

Nicklaus is incredulous, and he says to Stevie Wonder: "We must play a game sometime."

Wonder replies: "Well, people don't take me seriously so I only play when there's money on the line, and actually I never play for less than $100,000 a hole."

Nicklaus thinks about it and says "OK, I am game for that. When would you like to play?"

Stevie Wonder turns around and says, "Well, just about any night suits me."

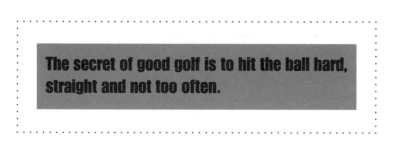

The secret of good golf is to hit the ball hard, straight and not too often.

If you live in a climate where intense heat prohibits you from maximizing your practice time, then consider a Port-A-Cool. It's the portable cooling system you see on the sidelines at many National Football League games.

There are seven different models to choose from, ranging in price from $1,099 to $2,400. The company claims that it costs just 50 cents a day to operate a cooler.

Put it in your back yard chipping area or next to your stall on the driving range. It will lower the temperature by 20 degrees or more.

For more information, call Golf Depot at (888) 335-1137.

*O*nce there was a millionaire, who collected live alligators. He lived on the edge of an exclusive golf club and kept the alligators in the lake. The millionaire also had a beautiful daughter who was single. One day he decides to throw a huge party for the club's members, and during the party he announces, "My dear guests . . . I have a proposition to every man here. I will give one million dollars or my daughter to the man who can swim across this lake full of alligators and emerge unharmed!"

As soon as he finished his last word, there was the sound of a large SPLASH!! There was one guy in the lake swimming with all he could. The crowd cheered him on as he kept stroking. Finally, he made it to the other side unharmed. The millionaire was impressed.

He yelled to the other side of the lake, "My boy that was incredible! Fantastic! I didn't think it could be done! Well, I must keep my end of the bargain. Which do you want, my daughter or the million dollars?"

The guy yells back, "Listen, I don't want your money! And I don't want your daughter! I want the person who pushed me in the WATER!!!"

*O*ne mid-afternoon on a sunny day, a golfer teed up his ball. After a few practice swings, he steps up to his ball and gets ready to drive the first hole. Just before he swings, a woman in a wedding gown comes running up from the parking lot.

She has tears streaming down her face. Just as she reaches the raised tee, she screams out, "You bastard! I can't believe it! How could you do that?"

The golfer calmly takes a swing and drives the ball straight down the fairway.

He looks at the woman, as he puts his driver back in his bag and says, "Hey, I said only if it's raining."

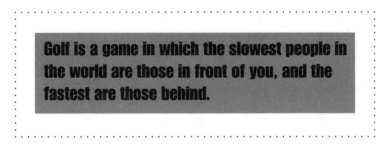

Golf is a game in which the slowest people in the world are those in front of you, and the fastest are those behind.

*S*tanding on the tee of a relatively long par-3, the confident golfer said to his caddie, "Looks like a 4-wood and a putt to me."

The caddie handed him the 4-wood, which he topped and sent the ball about 15 yards off the front of the tee.

Immediately the caddie handed him his putter and said, "And now for one hell of a putt."

To add to the golfing look of your home, check out Best Value Golf Products of Brandon, Florida.

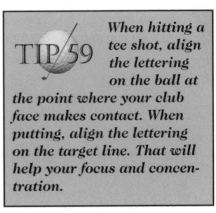

When hitting a tee shot, align the lettering on the ball at the point where your club face makes contact. When putting, align the lettering on the target line. That will help your focus and concentration.

Among its many products that are a must are a floor lamp, table lamp, magazine stand and an end table.

The floor lamp measures 64 inches high and is made of three genuine golf club shafts, club heads and golf balls. (The box claims that you can take the lamp apart and play a round with the clubs.) The shade comes in natural, green or black. The floor lamp sells for $189.95.

The table lamp also features three genuine golf club shafts, heads and balls, but measures only 32 inches high. The shade comes in natural, green or black. It sells for $129.95.

The magazine stand comes in black or chrome and uses two genuine drivers which have been bent in the shaft. Metal bars connect the two clubs and provide the space for more than a dozen magazines. It sells for $139.95.

The end table features a sturdy black powder coated or chrome steel tripod frame made of real clubs and golf balls. A tempered glass is kidney shaped ala a green. The table measures 23 inches by 16 inches and is two feet high. It sells for $159.95.

You can reach Best Value Golf by calling (813) 655-3626.

A man dies and approaches the pearly gates where he encounters St. Peter.

"Ah," says St. Peter. "We have been expecting you. I'd like to let you walk through the pearly gates here, and looking through my book, I notice you've lived a good life . . . but . . . I see that one time you got a little angry and said the 'F' word, didn't you?"

"Yes," says the man, "but it was only one time."

St. Peter said, "Well, I've been known to make an exception when there are extenuating circumstances."

So the man says, "Well, I said the 'F' word when I was playing golf!"

St. Peter said, "Oh, so you're a golfer, are you? Well that does explain a lot. Go ahead and tell me why you said the 'F' word."

The man began to explain. "Well, I was playing in a tournament, and I had a one-stroke lead. As I started into my back swing for my drive on the last hole, just at the peak of my swing, I realized that I had chosen the wrong club! I had the five iron instead of the four iron . . ."

St. Peter said, "Ah, and that's when you said the 'F' word?"

The man replied, "Well, no, as it turned out I hit the five-iron shot of my life! The ball was headed straight up the fairway, when all of a sudden, a passing bird flew right into the ball's path . . ."

So St. Peter said, "You said the 'F' word then, didn't you?"

"Well, no," the man continued. "Just as the bird got to the ball, it started to hook, and the bird actually helped direct the ball toward the green, where it landed and started to roll toward the cup! It was rolling real well, when all of a sudden, a squirrel came onto the green and came towards my ball. . ."

A very agitated St. Peter asked, "The 'F' word, you said it then, yes?"

The man replied, "Well, the squirrel actually pushed the ball toward the hole, where it stopped rolling just about two inches from the cup. . ."

To which St. Peter screamed, "YOU DIDN'T MISS THE F—ING PUTT, DID YOU?"

> **In days of old, when the tribe's leaders beat the ground with clubs and shrieked, it was called ritual. These days, we prefer to call it golf.**

*G*od and the devil decided to play a round of golf one day, just for the fun of it.

The devil drew honors on the first hole and hit a perfect drive 280 yards that split the fairway.

God teed up and hit an ugly duck hook that headed straight out of bounds into the woods. The ball bounced madly off one tree then another and then miraculously popped out high in the air back toward the fairway. Instead of landing safely in the fairway, however, the ball landed square on the back of a dove flying by. The dove carried the ball toward the green, 400 yards away. Unfortunately, the ball slipped off the dove's back into the water hazard just short of the green. No sooner had the ball plopped into the water when a giant water spout arose and lifted the ball up into the air, onto the green and into the cup for an ace.

The devil shook his head disgustedly and asked, "Do you want to play golf or do you want to screw around?"

hat is the perfect gift for the woman in your life who enjoys golf? How about a holiday basket filled with golf goodies, chosen especially for her?

Best Value Golf in Brandon, Florida, (813-655-3626) offers such a basket for $189. The wooden basket contains a pair of your choice of any style Lady Fairway golf shoes, golf glove, two pairs of golf socks, a cap, visor, cedar shoe trees, shoe horn and a collection of golf poetry.

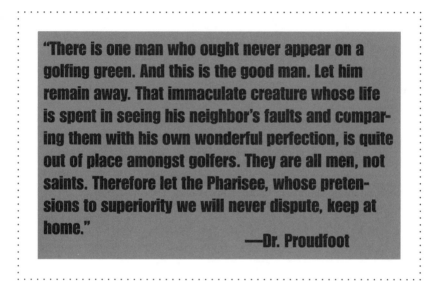

"There is one man who ought never appear on a golfing green. And this is the good man. Let him remain away. That immaculate creature whose life is spent in seeing his neighbor's faults and comparing them with his own wonderful perfection, is quite out of place amongst golfers. They are all men, not saints. Therefore let the Pharisee, whose pretensions to superiority we will never dispute, keep at home."

—Dr. Proudfoot

A young golf pro had just opened a new course. He'd built a beautiful pro shop and had it furnished with the finest golf equipment from around the world. Sitting there, one the fisrt day the shop was open, he saw a man come into the shop. Wishing to make a good first impression, the young pro picked up the telephone and started to pretend he was talking with Jack Nicklaus. He suggested several tips and pretended to record a tee time for the following week for Nicklaus. Finally, he hung up and asked the visitor, "Can I halp you?"

The man said, "Sure, I've come to install the phone!"

Drive for show, putt for dough, shank for comic relief.

There were three golfers at a 19th Hole bar. One man got drunk and started a fight with the other two men. The police came and took the drunk golfer to jail. The next day the man, an independently wealthy young retiree, went before the judge.

The judge asked the man, "Where do you work?"

The man said, "Here and there, but not really."

The judge asked the man, "What do you do for a living?"

The man said, "This and that, but not much."

The judge then said, "Take him away."

The man said, "Wait, judge, when will I get out? I have a 7:48 tee time in the morning."

The judge said to the man, "Sooner or later, but I'd bet on later."

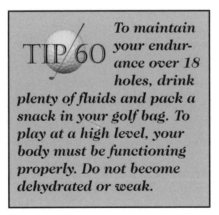

TIP 60 *To maintain your endurance over 18 holes, drink plenty of fluids and pack a snack in your golf bag. To play at a high level, your body must be functioning properly. Do not become dehydrated or weak.*

HOLE 14

Who says simulated computer golf games are too spacious and too expensive for the average golfer? Contact Dead Solid Golf of Pittston, Pennsylvania, at (800) 889-3727.

Dead Solid Golf has a portable inflatable version for sale, or rent it for special occasions. Besides 18-hole course competition, the simulator can conduct a longest drive or closest to the pin contest. You also can compete in the Lunar Long Drive Contest (with only 1/6 of the gravity on Earth).

The inflatable products include a Swing Analyzer, FaceTrac Swing Analysis, Full Course Play, Driving Range, Events Mode, Into the Screen Putting and a Power PC G3 Computer with CD-ROM.

Completely erected, the portable simulator is 20 feet long, 18 feet wide and 12 feet high.

Q: Why does a golfer bring an extra pair of socks to the course with him?

A: Just in case he gets a hole in one.

*S*cott was staying in a tiny hotel on a small Caribbean island and decided to play a round of golf at the local club course.

He was assigned a caddie who carried the bag over one shoulder and a gun over the other.

Scott, a little unsettled by seeing the rifle, hooked his first tee shot into the rough. When he went to take his second shot, an alligator charged him, but quick as a flash, the caddie shot the animal dead in his tracks.

On the second tee, Scott again drove into the rough, where another alligator darted out to attack him. Once again, the caddie shot in the nick of time.

On the third hole, Scott's iron shot from the fairway rolled into the mud right next to a sleeping alligator. Scott looked expectantly at his caddie, who made no move to unshoulder the rifle.

"Aren't you going to take care of the alligator?" asked Scott.

The caddie shook his head, "No extra shots on a par 3."

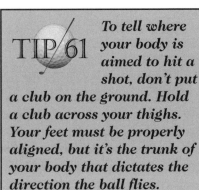

TIP 61

To tell where your body is aimed to hit a shot, don't put a club on the ground. Hold a club across your thighs. Your feet must be properly aligned, but it's the trunk of your body that dictates the direction the ball flies.

*L*earn proper alignment and tempo by utilizing the Ultimate Tempo Golf Swing Regulator. It is a mat and pad combination, built with recycled materials, that gives the feeling of swinging through grass.

Strategic markings on the regulator are established to instill a successful method for consistent alignment of the shot, proper set up to the target path, and a dynamic method for a tempo oriented golf swing that will enable the player to make consistently accurate golf shots. Use it indoors with plastic balls or outdoors on the driving range with real balls. The design allows usage of every club in the bag, including your putter.

The mat is available for $139.99 from Renaissance International Golf Unlimited of Revere, Massachusetts, at (781) 284-6462.

> **"I can airmail the golf ball, but sometimes I don't put the right address on it."**
>
> **—Jim Dent**

*W*atching from the clubhouse overlooking the 18th green, the crowd saw a foursome on its way up.

Having marked their balls, suddenly one of the guys fell down and the three others started a fist fight.

The golf captain stormed out from the clubhouse to separate the fighters.

"What the hell's this all about?" he demanded of the foursome.

Said one: "My partner had a stroke and died just now, and these idiots want to include it on the scorecard."

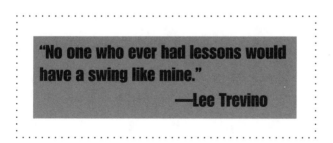

> **"No one who ever had lessons would have a swing like mine."**
>
> **—Lee Trevino**

A man was playing golf one day, and he hit his ball deep into the rough.

As he was searching for his ball he happened to find a bottle laying in the grass and when he picked it up, a great genie appeared.

"This is terrific," the man said. "Does this mean that I get three wishes granted?"

"Yes," replied the genie, "But be careful, for whatever you wish your wife will get 10 times greater."

So, the man thought and he finally said, "Make me the best golfer at the club."

The genie told him, "You will be the best male golfer at the club, but your wife will be 10 times better."

"OK," he said, "Give me a million dollars."

The genie replied, "It is granted, but your wife now has 10 million dollars."

The genie said, "You have only one wish left, so use it wisely."

The man replied, "Give me a slight heart attack."

TIP 62 *On short downhill putts concentrate on the line. The ball will get to the hole, so take your time getting the right line.*

T ired of collecting logo golf balls? Then start collecting ball markers or golf pencils.

For just $39.95 you can get a solid black walnut frame with suede cloth base that holds up to 50 ball marks. It has a back-stand for desktop display and an attachable brass plate for you to engrave. It measures 8 x 14 inches and is kidney shaped like a golf green.

For the same price, you can get a walnut or oak display that holds up to 80 golf pencils. It has felt backing and is ready to hang. It measures 21 x 15 inches.

Both displays are available from Golf Day of Revere, Massachusetts, at (800) 669-8600.

> **"Let's see, I think right now I'm third on the money-winning list and first in money-spending."**
>
> **—Tony Lema**

The Peace Missile Corporation of San Rafael, California, has come up with a unique driver and putter. No, it isn't touting the shape or design. It is using construction material as the main selling point.

The Peace Missile Driver II's head is made from Russian and U.S. nuclear ballistic missile parts (Soviet SS-23 and Polaris A-3) that are mixed with other metals to form one of the strongest and lightest metals known to man. (The top secret metal has a patent pending.)

Endorsed by TV star Lyle Waggoner and long-ball champ Cary Schuman, the driver comes with a graphite shaft in various lengths, but only 10.5 degrees of loft.

It sells for $199.

The same company also makes the Peace Putter, made of the same metal compound. It also sports a Russian titanium shaft and is available in three different lengths. It sells for $79.

For more information, call (800) 700-1211.

A Marine drill sergeant fancied a round of golf one day, and headed out to his favorite links. Waiting on the first tee, he noticed an Air Force commander, also waiting on the first tee and also alone.

TIP/63 *Ben Hogan was asked, "What are the three most important clubs in the bag?" His reply? The driver, putter and wedge. Spend a good portion of your practice time on those three clubs and you soon will see your scores drop.*

Both being in the Armed Forces, they decided to play together.

It wasn't long before they were talking about work. They shared boot camp stories, war memories and jokes about new recruits. It went this way until about the third hole, when the Marine sergeant was finishing a story about a runaway tank and said, "And you know that the Marines are the bravest men in the Armed Forces."

The Air Force commander dropped his putter. "Just what do you mean by that?" he challenged.

"Well," the sergeant went on, "who do you send to take new territory? Who do you send in when you're outnumbered? Who gets the call for the most covert operations?"

The Air Force commander putted out, and angrily said, "Well, while you are hiding in the bushes, who is a clear target in the sky? Who do you call for support when you're losing? And who is always sent in during a losing battle? Sir, the men of the Air Force are the bravest men."

This argument lasted for the rest of the round. Both men swearing their men were the bravest, and each had stories to tell to back up their claims.

After finishing, they headed to the clubhouse for a beer, still debating the matter. Finally, the Marine sergeant stood and said, "I've got to head back to camp. Play again next week?"

To this, the Air Force commander said, "Well, I must apologize. It seems I was mistaken. Anyone who played like you did today, and is willing to come back to the same golf course is a much braver man than I."

*T*he barber was cutting hair one day when a guy comes into his shop with a bandage around his neck. He asks the man what happened.

In a low raspy voice he said, "Yesterday, I was playing golf with my mother-in-law. On the second hold she sliced her ball way over into a cow-pasture. She really hates to lose a ball, so we looked, and we looked, and we looked. There was no ball in sight. Just an old ugly cow. She screamed, 'I'm not leaving till I find that ball.'

"After another useless search I passed by the cow and decided, 'what the hell'—so I lifted the cow's tail and sure enough there was a ball stuck there.

"I called my mother-in-law over and said, 'Does this look like yours?' Well, she hit me in the throat with a 7 iron . . ."

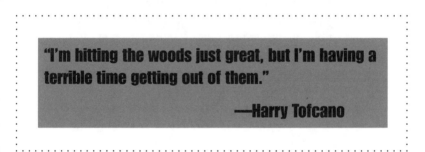

"I'm hitting the woods just great, but I'm having a terrible time getting out of them."

—Harry Tofcano

HOLE 15

S ometimes being noticed on a crowded golf course is desirous. You can accomplish it with knickers, a flamboyant hat or an incredibly smooth swing. However, the surest way to be noticed on the course is to drive around in a Classic Golf Car. As the manufacturer's ads say, "You don't drive an ordinary car to your office, so why settle for ordinary 'carts' at the links?"

The Classic Cars include reproductions of a 1932 Roadster, a 1936 Stepside, a 1934 Landau and a 1932 Phaeton. Each car is built to order, allowing customers to select their own color, fabrics and drive train options.

Prices vary, so contact Classic Car Company in Princeton, Minnesota, at (612) 389-9139. It also customizes golf carts to resemble hot rods or company vehicles.

A husband and wife were out enjoying a round of golf, and about to tee off on the third hole lined with beautiful homes.

The wife hit her shot and the ball began to slice; her shot was headed directly at a very large plate-glass window. Much to her surprise, the ball smashed through the window and shattered it into a million pieces.

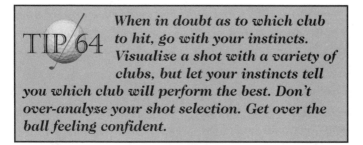

TIP/64 When in doubt as to which club to hit, go with your instincts. Visualize a shot with a variety of clubs, but let your instincts tell you which club will perform the best. Don't over-analyze your shot selection. Get over the ball feeling confident.

They felt compelled to see what damage was done and drove off to see what happened. When they peeked inside the house, they found no one there.

The husband called out and no one answered. Upon further investigation, they saw a gentleman sitting on the couch with a turban on his head.

The wife asked the man, "Do you live here?"

"No, someone just hit a ball through the window, knocked over the vase you see there, freeing me from that little bottle. I am so grateful!" he answered.

The wife asked, "Are you a genie?"

"Oh, why yes I am. In fact, I am so grateful I will grant you two wishes, and the third I will keep for myself," the genie replied.

The husband and wife agreed on two wishes; one was for a scratch handicap for the husband, to which the wife readily agreed. The other was for an income of $1,000,000 per year forever.

The genie nodded his head and said, "Done!"

The genie then said, "For my wish, I would like to have my way with your wife. I have not been with a woman for many years, and after all, I made you a scratch golfer and a millionaire."

The husband and wife agreed. After the genie and wife were finished, the genie asked the wife, "How long have you been married?" To which she responded, "Three years." The genie then asked, "How old is your husband?" To which she replied, "31 years old."

The genie then asked, "And how long has he believed in this genie stuff?"

*A*reknown golf trick shot artist was held in high regard by his caddie, who watched in awe at every exhibition while his boss would easily hit balls from every stance any way that an onlooker requested.

Then one day the caddie approached the trick shot artist and asked if he was willing to switch roles for that days exhibition. The trick shot artist agreed and, for a while, the caddie handled himself remarkably well, hitting golf balls off one foot and using his putter as a driver.

When it came time for requests from onlookers, a man in the back yelled, "Can you hit a ball 300 yards standing on one foot, blindfolded, using the back of your 7 iron?"

"That is an extremely simple shot," he responded. "So simple, in fact, that even my caddie can hit it, which is exactly what he will do."

Golf is an expensive way of playing marbles.

*W*hen your club face gets dirty, you probably wet a towel and wipe the face clean. You might even use a tee to dig out some dirt and grass from the grooves. That is good enough for weekend golfers, but if you are serious about your game, then get serious about your club cleaning.

Golf Coast Ultrasonics in New Port Richey, Florida, has developed a cleaning process that is unmatched. Ultrasonic energy consists of vibrations or sound waves above the frequencies normally heard by the human ear. The vibrations are produced by special equipment consisting of an ultrasonic generator that produces high frequency alternating electrical current and a transducer that transforms the high frequency into mechanical vibrations.

The vibrations are transmitted into liquids consisting of either water based or solvent-type chemicals that, in turn, contact the surfaces to be cleaned. Millions of microscopic bubbles are produced, and they implode, resulting in the production of extremely small, but highly intense shock waves. Because of the size of the shock waves and the volume of implosions, the cleansing action penetrates every spot on the submerged club face.

The process also can be used to clean the clubs' grips, removing every bit of sweat, body oil, sand and dirt.

The good news? It only takes about three minutes to clean a whole set of clubs.

The bad news? It isn't cheap, and it isn't portable.

For more information, call (727) 372-0392.

Willie Nelson, the country music singer, recently purchased a large golf course in the middle of Texas. He was being interviewed by the local TV station one day and was asked how each hole's par was determined.

He said, "That's easy. I own the course, it can be any par I want. Take that hole over there for instance, it is a par-46 and yesterday I birdied it."

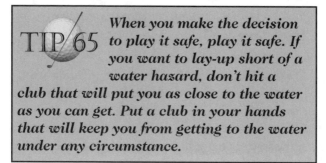

TIP 65 When you make the decision to play it safe, play it safe. If you want to lay-up short of a water hazard, don't hit a club that will put you as close to the water as you can get. Put a club in your hands that will keep you from getting to the water under any circumstance.

or the sports fan on your shopping list, consider a custom golf bag with his or her favorite college, National Football League, National Basketball Association, National Hockey League or Major League Baseball team logo on the side.

Terry Roy Custom Golf Bag Outfitters uses top-of-the-line Belding Sports golf bags, then customizes them with the team of your choice. Prices range from $300 to $450. Matching head covers are available, too.

Terry Roy is based in Charleston, Illinois, and can be reached by calling (800) 790-8769.

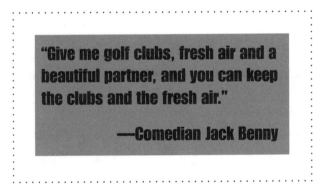

"Give me golf clubs, fresh air and a beautiful partner, and you can keep the clubs and the fresh air."

—Comedian Jack Benny

There was a golf course that specialized in senior-citizen caddies. After completing a round, the starter asked one golfer, "So, how did the caddie work out?"

The man replied, "He was nice enough, but he couldn't see far enough to follow the ball."

"I'm sorry," said the starter, "Come back next week and I'll be sure you get a caddie that can see far enough."

The next week the man showed up and the starter introduced him to his 80-year-old caddie.

"Are you sure he can see?" asked the man.

"Absolutely," said the starter.

So off they went to the first tee. The man hit his drive and said to the caddie, "Did you see that?"

"I sure did," came the reply.

They walked together down the fairway and the man said to the caddie, "Well, where did my ball go?"

The caddie replied, "What ball?"

I f you are tired of all those animal head covers, then get a set of The Three Stooges Talking Head Covers.

That's right. Just press their hands for a humorous one liner. Each stooge has two unique lines. They are appropriately attired in authentic-looking golf wear.

There are Larry, Moe and Curley head covers and they are $29.95 each. Batteries not included.

To order, call Golf Day of Revere, Massachusetts, at (800) 669-8600.

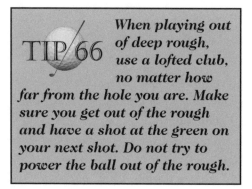

TIP 66

When playing out of deep rough, use a lofted club, no matter how far from the hole you are. Make sure you get out of the rough and have a shot at the green on your next shot. Do not try to power the ball out of the rough.

*T*wo *Scotsmen, Sandy and Angus, were playing golf one day and came upon a water hole.*

Sandy hit and sent one into the middle of the pond. He reached into his bag and found that he had no balls remaining.

He asked Angus for a ball and promptly hit that one into the pond as well. That goes on three of four more times, and when he asks Angus for a sixth ball, Angus says, "Sandy, these balls cost me a lot of money."

To which Sandy replies, "Angus, lad, if you can't afford to play the game, you should not be out here."

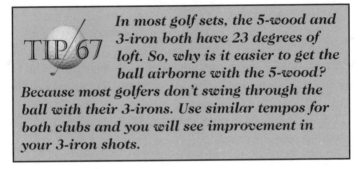

TIP 67 In most golf sets, the 5-wood and 3-iron both have 23 degrees of loft. So, why is it easier to get the ball airborne with the 5-wood? Because most golfers don't swing through the ball with their 3-irons. Use similar tempos for both clubs and you will see improvement in your 3-iron shots.

HOLE 16

If a sore back keeps you from bending over to fix your ball marks on the greens, then you must get The Green Fix Grip.

For just $7.90 from Down Pat Golf Company of Brookings, Oregon, you can clip a small hinged ball mark repairer to the end of your putter's grip. Snap up the prongs, turn your putter upside down and fix your ball mark without bending over. Snap the prongs back into place and no one knows they are there.

Down Pat also offers the unique Chipinski Golf Umbrella. In rainy weather, it looks and works like any golf umbrella. However, in good weather the umbrella easily inverts and can be used as a catcher of chips, putts or pitch shots. It's available in a variety of colors and can be customized with your company's logo. The base price is $39.95 each.

For more information on The Green Fix Grip or Chipinski Golf Umbrella, call (800) 993-9344.

*P*utts: What golfers attempt to sink on the green.

*P*utz: The guy who, to his own benefit, records the wrong score.

> **"A golfer rarely needs to hit a spectacular shot unless the one that precedes it was pretty bad."**
>
> **—Harvey Penick**

A woman is cleaning out her attic and comes across a small box. She opens it and finds three golf balls and $250.

When her husband comes home she questions him, and he finally admits that every time he was unfaithful to her he put a golf ball in the box.

She immediately goes ballistic and starts yelling at him, but as she is doing so she thinks, 30 years of marriage and only three golf balls?

She calms down and says, "What you have done is not nice, but I'll forgive you. However, I still don't know what the $250 is all about."

Her husband looks up at her and timidly says, "Well darling, every time I had collected a dozen balls I would sell them."

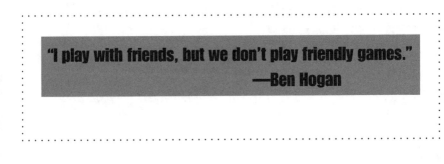

> **"I play with friends, but we don't play friendly games."**
> **—Ben Hogan**

Do you ever wonder where to get those cards and markers for recording the leaders of longest drive and closest to the pin contests? Wonder no more.

LaMond Golf in Painesville, Ohio, makes Skin Shot proximity markers. The markers come in two sizes (12-inches or 24-inches high) and six different colors. They can be customized with logos, pictures, business cards, etc. They have acrylic writing surfaces that can be cleaned after each use. A refillable grease pencil is attached to the writing surface.

The 12-inch model sells for $10; the 24-incher is $12. For more information, call (440) 352-4800.

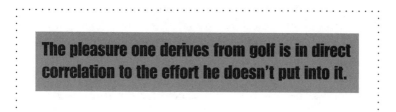

The pleasure one derives from golf is in direct correlation to the effort he doesn't put into it.

A wife begins to get a little worried because her husband has not arrived home on time from his regular Saturday afternoon golf game.

As the hours pass she becomes more and more concerned until at 8 p.m. the husband finally pulls into the driveway.

"What happened?" says the wife. "You should have been home hours ago!"

"Dave had a heart attack at the third hole," replied the husband.

"Oh, that's terrible." says the wife. "I know," the husband answers.

"All day long it was hit the ball, drag Dave, hit the ball, drag Dave . . . "

> ## TIP 68
>
> *If you have a choice, hire a caddie rather than use a golf cart. Caddies do more than carry your clubs. A good caddie will provide you with distances to the hole, as well as exact pin locations. A great caddie also will help you maintain a good mental outlook on the game. And the walk will be better for you, too.*

It's called the Ugly Stick. However, the manufacturer claims that you'll call it the most beautiful club in your bag after hitting it. The oversized wood head is made of kevlar, an indestructible, incomparably hard synthetic material with applications in aeronautics and aerospace. The loft is 10.5 degrees; the lie is 53 degrees; the weight is 210 grams. The head has a unique gold metallic finish; the carbon graphite shaft is gloss black.

The Ugly Stick sells for $149.95 and is made by Pete Cousin in Virginia Beach, Virginia. For more information, call (757) 491-9201.

One day two software engineers were out playing a round of golf. They came to a par-3 with a blind tee shot. Both teed off and watched their ball sail toward the flag.

When they got to the green, one of the balls was perched on the lip of the cup and other was in. As it turned out, both were playing Titleist 3s.

A heated argument ensued and they finally decided to let the club pro sort the mess out.

The pro walked to the hole with them and looked at the ball on the green and then the ball in the hole.

He turned to the two players in disgust and asked, "OK. Which of you is playing the white ball and which is playing the orange ball?"

> **"I'm going to win so much money this year, my caddie will make the top twenty money-winners list."**
>
> **—Lee Trevino**

*W*hat's the difference between golfing in New York and golfing in Canada?
In New York they say, "Eh, get off the green!"
In Canada they say, "Get off the green, eh?"

*G*olf Training Aids.Com sells a number of instructional devices on the Internet. Among the most unique training aids it offers are:

"TacTic." This product has found enormous popularity among golf schools whose students find its definitive feedback very appealing. Strap it on your leading hand like a watch. If you break your wrists at the top of the swing, or at impact, the TacTic goes CLICK and you know it's time to try again. It works for right- or left-handed players and for every club in the bag. ($29.95)

"High-Tech Putting Track." The inconsistent and unreliable feedback that comes from conventional putting practice makes it very difficult to truly improve your stroke without the use of appropriate learning aids. The Putting Track combines kinesthetic and visual feedback.

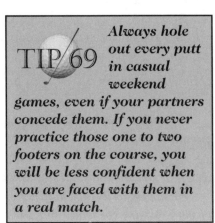

TIP 69

Always hole out every putt in casual weekend games, even if your partners concede them. If you never practice those one to two footers on the course, you will be less confident when you are faced with them in a real match.

The PVC rails can be adjusted to be slightly wider than your putter head, and when your stoke is off line, the putter will hit one of the rails, giving you automatic feedback. A bright yellow string above the track gives additional feedback about path and face angle, while colored beads on the guideline and the measured reference lines on the rail can help teach length of stoke and acceleration. ($49.95)

"Touch Putting Board." This new trainer allows you to master the three-foot putt with just a little practice. It reduces the size of the hole to three inches for more difficulty and to increase your accuracy. This will make the holes on the course seem larger. The downhill angle gives you practice on those touchy speed putts. ($59.95).

"Putting Trainer." It fits any standard putter and teaches the mechanics of the square-to-square or pendulum stroke used by the best putters in the world. Continued use of the Trainer reinforces and maintains proper mechanics. It also includes an instructional video. ($14.95)

"Power Coil." The Coil is designed to stabilize a player's base and develop a powerful coiling action, thus increasing the potential for increased distance. Anyone who has a problem swaying back away from the target or locking the back leg at the top of the swing can benefit from strapping on the Power Coil. ($49.95)

"Swing Gyde." This is a simple, but effective product designed to teach you a better take away, as well as how and where to set the wrists during the swing. The device assures a proper set at the top of the swing, a better swing arc and swing plane. The Gyde also helps with set up and alignment to the target. ($34.95)

"Golfer Rx." This comprehensive score analysis system allows golfers to track every detail of their rounds by providing charts and graphs based upon user input. The CD-ROM can help you analyze your scores and your shots. Analysis for up to four different golfers. Requires IBM compatible computer with Windows 95 and a CD-ROM drive. ($29.95)

"Golfercize." This golf fitness system packs easily in a briefcase, attaches to any door hinge and takes strokes off any game. The 235-page manual explains the biomechanics of a golf swing and recommends more than 200 stretching and strengthening routines. ($69.95)

"Gary Player Golf Gym." Gary Player calls it the best golf specific exercise/swing development program he has ever used. The Golf Gym

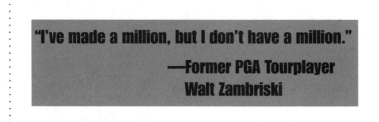

"I've made a million, but I don't have a million."

—Former PGA Tourplayer
Walt Zambriski

has molded grips to help you grip the "club" correctly. You learn to feel the perfect golf swing. Includes a demonstration video, exercise chart and travel bag. ($49.95)

"PVC Mirror." This PVC framed practice mirror allows monitoring of all positions of the swing. It has a large 2-feet by 4-feet surface area with minimal distortion and has the added benefit of two adjustable lines which can be set to visually guide your swing plane or specifically check your positions. The mirror folds flat for easy storage and can be used indoors or out. ($199.95)

"Bushnell Rangefinder 600." This product uses lasers to measure distances. It is about half the size of other laser rangefinder models and easily fits in a jacket pocket. It utilizes a scan mode that allows the player to find the distance of multiple target as they are viewed. While in scan mode, the player can differentiate the flag from other objects quite easily. ($499.95)

"Drivetime Driving Range." You swing. It catches it, shags it and tees it. The tubular steel frame, quick fold design, all-weather net is ideal for indoor or back yard practice. It weighs just 24.95 pounds, so it is easy to move. ($237.45)

"If you travel first class, you think first class and you are more likely to play first class."

—Senior PGA Tour
player Ray Floyd

"Ray Floyd's ShotMaster." This easy to use practice and training device places 30 years of Raymond Floyd's professional experiences in the palm of your hand. Simply enter the conditions of the shot using multiple choice menus and the ShotMaster graphically shows you exactly how to best hit the shot. ($79.95)

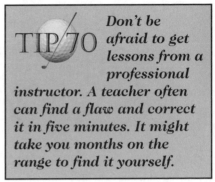

TIP 70 *Don't be afraid to get lessons from a professional instructor. A teacher often can find a flaw and correct it in five minutes. It might take you months on the range to find it yourself.*

To order any of these items, go to golftrainingaids.com on the Internet or call (800) 723-7851.

Two women are playing golf when one of them asks the other, "Do you and your husband have mutual climax?" The other woman replies, "No, I think we have State Farm."

HOLE 17

Gary Player also offers the Heavy Hitter. It's a weighted driver that helps build strength, as well as better swing tempo. The club is designed with a perimeter weighted club head, matched to a weighted shaft that flexes perfectly for a natural ball flight trajectory.

It comes in three different weights (from 650 to 1,000 grams) and is available with a training grip or for left-handed players. There also is an iron version.

The clubs sell for $89 (driver) and $79 (iron) and are available at (888) 88-HEAVY.

Barry was playing at a municipal course adjacent to the town zoo. Slicing his first tee shot into the lion cage, Barry walked over to the fence. The lone lion was asleep in the shade on the far side of the cage. Barry saw his ball about 10 feet from the lion.

He thought, "That's the ball my wife gave me for our anniversary. She'll never forgive me if I lose it on the very first shot."

So, Barry wriggled between the bars into the cage. Being careful not to wake the lion, Barry crawled slowly to his ball. He was just about ready to grab it when an impatient player in the following

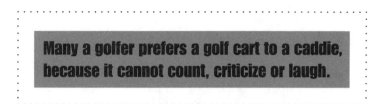

Many a golfer prefers a golf cart to a caddie, because it cannot count, criticize or laugh.

group hit an errant shot off the first tee. The player yelled "Fore!" and woke up the lion.

The lion took one look at Barry in the cage and leaped to its feet. Barry began running, but slipped and fell. Barry was too scared to move. The lion began circling Barry, getting closer and closer with each revolution. His hopes of survival were dim. Barry got on his knees, opened his arms and said, "My God! Please give this lion some religion!"

Then, there was lightning in the air and the lion stopped just a foot short of Barry. The lion was puzzled and looked up in the air and said, "My God! Thank you for the food I am about to receive. . ."

"Lessons are not to take the place of practice, but to make practice worthwhile."
—Harvey Penick

ne of the best catalogs for finding unique golf gifts and gadgets is The Golfsmith Store. To obtain a catalog, or order any of these items, call (800) 396-0099.

Hole-in-One Wall Plaque, $69.95.
Men's Golf Slippers, $24.95.
Golf Park Bench, $169.95.
Screen Saver Set, $19.95.
Trivia Links Game, $24.95.
Golfer's Fireplace Set, $129.95.

Masters Card Collection, $29.95.
Foot Magnets, $29.95.
Electric Golf Cart Heater, $129.95.
Golf Fisherman Ball Retriever, $14.95.
Laser Practice Pro Putter, $119.95.
Baby Golf Shoes, $16.95.
Golf Spike Sandals, $79.95.

Don't assume that the only productive practice is at the golf course. Putting can be improved on most home carpets. The grip and stance can be refined in front of a bedroom mirror. Tempo and rhythm can be practiced in a garage or backyard. Work on the little things at home and the ball striking will be easier at the range.

HOLE 18

Another outstanding source for golf gadgets and unique gifts is the Competitive Edge Golf catalog. To get a copy of the catalog or to order any of these items, call (800) 433-4465.

Pewter Wine Stoppers, $40.
Female Golfer Martini Glass, $24.
Green Marble PGA Pen, $29.95.
Animal Head Covers, $16.
Pocket Ball Washer, $2.99.
Hot Shot Ball Warmer, $39.
Half-Fingered Gloves, $8.95.
Backyard Flag Set, $34.
Golf Hypnosis Audio Tape, $14.95.
Bite Suede Golf Boots, $99.95.
Golfer's Hat Rack, $30.
Fossil Golf Watch, $69.
Club ID Labels, $7.95.

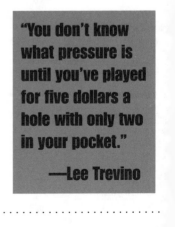

"You don't know what pressure is until you've played for five dollars a hole with only two in your pocket."

—Lee Trevino

When chipping, to prevent the right hand from passing the left too soon, curl your left hand under in your grip.

TIP 72

*D*o you know who in 1923 was. . .
　　1. President of the largest steel company?
　　2. President of the largest gas company?
　　3. President of the New York Stock Exchange?
　　4. Greatest wheat speculator?
　　5. President of the Bank of International Settlement?
　　6. Great Bear of Wall Street?

These men should have been considered some of the world's most successful men. At least they found the secret of making money.

Now more than seven decades later, do you know what has become of these men?

1. The president of the largest steel company, Charles Schwab, died a pauper.

2. The president of the largest gas company, Edward Hopson, is insane.

3. The president of the N.Y.S.E., Richard Whitney, was released from prison to die at home.

4. The greatest wheat speculator, Arthur Cooger, died abroad, penniless.

5. The president of the Bank of International Settlement shot himself.

6. The Great Bear of Wall Street, Cosabee Rivermore, committed suicide.

The same year, 1923, the winner of the most important golf championship, Gene Sarazan, won the U.S. Open and PGA Tournaments. In his later years, he was still playing golf and was solvent.

Conclusion: STOP WORRYING ABOUT BUSINESS AND START PLAYING GOLF!

*T*he president joined some friends on a golf outing.
When they got ready to tee off on hole No. 1, the chief executive removed his jacket and revealed that he had a pair of panties stuck to his arm. Nobody in the group had enough guts to ask about it, so they continued on and played 18.

When they finished and were seated in the 19th Hole, with drinks flowing in generous quantities, one among them summoned the courage to ask:

"Mr. President, what's the story on those panties you have on your arm?"

The president's retort? "Hey, it's a patch! I'm trying hard to quit, damnit!"

A nd finally, if the words "politically correct" are not part of your vocabulary, then consider The Slick Willie Golf Ball. Adorned with a likeness of Bill Clinton, each ball is stamped, "SLICK WILLIE, A Good Lie Guaranteed."

The balls sell for $26.95 a dozen from P.I. Marketing of Bixby, Oklahoma. For more information, call (800) 792-2557.